OVERSHADOWS

OVERSHADOWS

An Investigation into a Terrifying
Modern Canadian Haunting

Richard Palmisano

THE DUNDURN GROUP
TORONTO • OXFORD

Publisher: Anthony Hawke
Copy-editor: Michael Hodge
Design: Emma Kassirer
Printer: University of Toronto Press

National Library of Canada Cataloguing in Publication Data

Palmisano, Richard
Overshadows : an investigation into a terrifying modern Canadian haunting / Richard Palmisano.

ISBN 1-55002-473-6

1. Haunted houses—Ontario. I. Title.

BF1472.C3P34 2003   133.1'29713   C2003-903114-4

1   2   3   4   5   07   06   05   04   03

We acknowledge the support of the **Canada Council for the Arts** and the **Ontario Arts Council** for our publishing program. We also acknowledge the financial support of the **Government of Canada** through the **Book Publishing Industry Development Program** and **The Association for the Export of Canadian Books,** and the **Government of Ontario** through the **Ontario Book Publishers Tax Credit** program, and the **Ontario Media Development Corporation's Ontario Book Initiative.**

Care has been taken to trace the ownership of copyright material used in this book. The author and the publisher welcome any information enabling them to rectify any references or credit in subsequent editions.

J. Kirk Howard, President

Printed and bound in Canada.⊕
Printed on recycled paper.

www.dundurn.com

Dundurn Press	Dundurn Press	Dundurn Press
8 Market Street	73 Lime Walk	2250 Military Road
Suite 200	Headington, Oxford,	Tonawanda NY
Toronto, Ontario, Canada	England	U.S.A. 14150
M5E 1M6	OX3 7AD	

OVERSHADOWS

acknowledgements

I would like to offer a sincere thank you to my family and friends, whose help and support made this book possible. Thanks to the following for all of their assistance and hard work: Paul, John, Catherine Jobe, Peter McSherry, the family who had to endure these events, and the investigative team members.

Thanks to the wonderful and talented people at Dundurn Press, and especially to Mr. Tony Hawke, whose wisdom taught me a great deal about the publishing business.

I would like to thank Mr. Dave Billingham at Odyctek for his support in my otherworldly adventures; you will always be my supplier of surveillance equipment and other fine gizmos. You helped me to see things that I normally wouldn't have seen.

A special thanks to my wife Michelle who, although she wanted to run away from this stuff, stood by my side and helped me get the job done.

I have been notified that the current owners of the property discussed in this book would like to remain anonymous; this includes the location of the property as well, as they feel that this story might hurt their business and inspire disruptive activities from the curious, which would destroy the privacy of the many people who live on the property. Although I do not give the address, I do attempt to give details of the surrounding area.

The people involved in the events described within have been given pseudonyms; however, this fact has no bearing on the validity of the story, or on the events which took place, nor does it alter the testimony of the witnesses. Furthermore, this secrecy has no reflection on the tape recordings or photographs accumulated during the investigation.

Anyone wishing to contact me for use of my information in their research may do so at: overshadows@sympatico.ca

table of contents

introduction

Imagine for a moment that you are in the safety of your own home, in the comfort of your own bed. It's late, and it has been a long day. You turn out the night light and prepare to sleep, when out of the darkness you hear footsteps in the hall, just beyond your bedroom door; they are heavy, deliberate, and approaching quickly. At first you hesitate with fear, then your survival instinct kicks in and pushes you to react. You reach for the light, switching it on just as the intruder arrives at your door. As the door arches open, the light from the lamp chases the darkness away and you can clearly see that there is nothing in the hall. You feel an uneasy relief but the fear remains, as you know that the intruder in your home has been dead for a very long time, and its intentions are completely unknown.

What can you do when your home is invaded by an unwanted and uninvited ghost? You have nowhere to go, and no desire to move. You stand your ground, quietly and desperately trying to make sense of it all, coping with it on a day-to-day basis, seized with terror by every noise. It plays heavily on your nerves, tearing away at your sanity. You desperately work at making it as normal a home as any. It isn't easy for those who find themselves faced with these phenomena; phenomena which have frightened, yet intrigued, people for centuries, and which seem to be on an increase. This book examines the terrifying events that have plagued one family and tries to find out why spirits continue to walk among us.

Hauntings, ghosts, and poltergeists; countless reports of sightings, occurrences, and strange happenings span dozens of generations and can even be traced back to the dawn of civilization. People in every walk of life report these events, from judges to factory workers, from homemakers to political leaders, but the questions for most people still exist: is there life after death? do souls wander among us? and if so, why? With the beginning of the new millennium we are seeing an interest in the paranormal to such an extent that it surpasses that which was demonstrated during the spiritual movement of the Victorian Era. It's uncertain if this renewed interest is due to the arrival of the new millennium, or if it is because of a noted and recorded rise in paranormal activity. People are not only more aware of their environment, but with today's electronic avenues of media and information, stories and activities are quickly relayed and associated, allowing the individual to seek out important questions regarding life after death. The hereafter has always been one of our greatest mysteries.

This book will examine the existence of life after death. Throughout this process, one must remember that when discussing the paranormal, and more specifically ghosts, there are three distinct categories of people. The first is the non-believer, who will maintain that there are no such things, and will regard witness statements or evidence as rubbish. This group will have an explanation for everything, even when an event is scientifically investigated and all naturally occurring phenomena have been discounted, leaving only the mystery. They will put it down to some natural activity that science has yet to discover.

Secondly, there is the believer who, through historical events, testimony, and possibly actual experience, has come to learn that anything is possible.

Finally, there is the skeptic. Healthy skepticism is a good tool, and used wisely it can enable one to differentiate between fact and fiction, truth and fabrication. However, skepticism has to be balanced. Too much and the world becomes impossible; scientific and social developments fall into a void, goals and dreams are never pursued because they can't possibly be reached. Too little skepticism and we become gullible; reality becomes distorted, lies and truth become intertwined and indistinguishable.

When truly looking into the possibility of life after death, we must have some knowledge of scientific principles and methods, and maintain a healthy skepticism at all times.

Regardless of what progress is made, or what evidence is brought forth, there will always be those who will choose not to believe, and that is their choice. After all, the question of life after death will always remain a personal one.

chapter 1

1995: A woman was sprawled out on the couch. You could see by the flicker of candlelight that her eyes were glazed over, transfixed into an unblinking stare at the images flashing on the television in the corner of the room. Its audio was drowned out by the rock music on the stereo. A syringe dropped from her hand, and upon landing a dribble of blood mixed with narcotics spilled to the floor from its point.

A shadow in the chair next to the couch stirred, leaned forward, and tossed an empty beer bottle haphazardly onto the coffee table. The shadow advanced to the woman and was met with total oblivion. He shifted her body; it was devoid of any physical or mental activity. Aside from her laboured breathing, she seemed dead. He remembered the conversation that they had had a few hours before, when they first met at the tavern down the street. "Why don't you come over to party, for a good time," she had asked him.

He got up and headed for the front door, looking back at her there on the couch, drool seeping from the corner of her mouth. He turned again, but instead of heading out the front door, he crept up the stairs that led to the second floor. He stood in the darkened hallway outside the bedroom door listening, waiting. He pushed the door open and stepped into the room, blocking the exit. She jumped up, startled to face this intruder, her scrapbook falling to the floor. He stepped in closer, pushing the door closed behind him, and began to disrobe.

> *"Take your pants off!"*
> *"Oh God"*
> *Struggling*
> *A slap*
> *Sobbing, "Oh Go...God"*
> *Excerpt from surveillance tape.*

She was fifteen, a beautiful outgoing young girl with everything to live for. Her neighbours knew her, although not well. They would exchange hellos and have casual conversations. They knew her pleasant smile, her love for animals, and some of her friends.

About a year earlier, they had moved into the servant's residence of an old manor that was built in the 1930s, and converted into a town-home in the 1950s. The young girl fell in love with its charm. Its archways, spacious rooms, and hardwood floors gave the old place character. Its location seemed perfect, surrounded by parks and gardens; it was only a hundred yards to Lake Ontario. She hoped that happiness would be found there.

She lived there with her mother, who was an abuser of drugs and alcohol, and was well known by the local police. The mother would bring strange men home from the local taverns, and the girl would suffer horrendous physical and sexual assaults at the hands of some of these men as her mother lay unconscious from her over-indulgence. She had endured much in her short life, and her character grew strong, but she was never mean-spirited. She always had a quick smile. She loved her pets and her friends, which were her only connections to sanity, and through it all she maintained an unconditional love for her mother. She knew things could be so much better for them if her mother didn't do the things she did. She was the adult, the role model; she was supposed to pass on her wisdom, support, and knowledge of life's pitfalls, not drag her into a pit.

One day, a letter was delivered to their door. It contained bad news. It stated that several months' back-rent were due, and that eviction proceedings had been started. This was no surprise to her mother, as she was no stranger to moving. It was, however, a crushing blow to the young girl. She didn't want to leave the house that she now loved. She grew angry with her mother for letting this happen, and decided that it was time to teach her a lesson.

She had tried to get her mother to change many times before, with no positive response — just a lot of talk and broken promises. Her plan seemed simple enough: overdosing on some of her mother's pills, being discovered and taken to the hospital, and getting the doctors and police involved in her very loud and desperate cry for help would not only scare her mother, but it would also give her a taste of what she had been making her daughter live with. They would be forced into counselling, and her mother would get the help that she so desperately needed.

Unfortunately, there was a flaw in the plan; it was a simple oversight, but what was undoubtedly the most critical piece of the plan was not thought of, and was therefore missing from the equation. There was no one there to discover her, and that night she died.

Shortly thereafter, the eviction was upheld and the sheriff sealed the doors. A few days later, a group of the girl's friends set out on an adventure. Some thought that this would allow them a chance to say a quiet good-bye to their sorely missed friend. Others thought that they might even be able to contact her through the veil of death. They stepped from the bus and slowly walked the block to her old house, stopping briefly in front of it. Fear overtook a couple of them in that instant, so they continued onto the park overlooking the lake. They discussed why they had come this far, and tried to build each other's courage. They went over their strategy for getting into the house, then finally moved back up the road, heading around the house to the rear alley. They helped each other climb up onto an adjacent roof, which would lead them directly to her bedroom window. It was found unlocked and they entered. The group assembled in her old bedroom. They sat in the cold dark house with little more than the light of a couple of candles they had brought with them. They huddled together around the Ouija board and attempted to make contact with their departed friend. Only the individuals present know the results of what happened that night; they fled the house in panic.

chapter 2

1996: It was the spring, and they had been dating for almost a year when they decided to move in together. Kellie worked from home and was raising a six-year-old daughter, Hailey, and Al worked for a property developer. He was fifteen years her senior, and they were both divorced. They began looking for a suitable place to live. Location was an important issue because his job required him to remain nearby at all times, they did not want to relocate the child to another school district, and they both had friends and family in the community.

The search began. They heard of a townhouse that had recently become available next door to some of Al's friends. They toured the house and instantly fell in love with it. Al was a collector of antiques, and could easily picture their furnishings there. Its old charm and spacious rooms were perfect, and it was located very close to where they presently lived. They had to have it. The property manager agreed, and they moved in right away.

With all of their belongings now in the house, there came the long arduous task of unpacking — finding that perfect place for pictures, furniture, and lamps. They were in their bedroom putting away clothing and odds and ends when they heard a noise on the stairs. They knew that they were alone in the house, but there was definitely someone coming up the stairs; the distinct footfalls were followed by the boards creaking under someone's weight. They went down the long hall and peered down the stairs, but no one was there. They went downstairs to the main floor to investigate. No one was found and the doors were locked.

The next day, my wife Shelby went over to help set up Hailey's bedroom and playroom. After several hours' work, they decided that it was time for a break. As Shelby left the playroom, heading for the stairs, a movement caught her attention in the bedroom. She looked in and saw the rocking chair in the corner of the room rocking by itself. It continued moving at a steady pace. She had been the last person in that room and the chair had been still when she left. She went downstairs and told Kellie about it. When Al arrived later, they told him what had happened. They all laughed, certain that there was a perfectly normal explanation, though no one offered any at the time.

The second incident that indicated that there may have been a problem in the house happened one day while Kellie sat in a room upstairs doing crafts. She froze with fear when she heard a group of people marching down the hall just outside the door. She inched her way to the door and peeked out. There was no one there, so she made a dash to the phone and called Al at work. He came home right away and checked the house, but there was no indication of anything out of the ordinary.

When they moved in, they had set up Hailey's bedroom in the small front room upstairs. Their neighbours had told them that the middle room used to belong to the deceased girl, so that room was utilized as a play area and craft room instead of a bedroom. Hailey was disturbed nightly; it was as if someone were pushing and poking her as she slept in the small room. This continued until they finally decided to switch the rooms, moving her bedroom into the middle room and putting her playthings in the front room. From the first night of that change she slept undisturbed.

However, Hailey had an old white china cabinet in her bedroom with two glass doors on the top section. It contained a collection of small porcelain dolls. The doors to the cabinet were constantly found open. Al and Kellie would snap them shut, only to find them open again later. Eventually, Al tied a cross in between the two door handles and they remained shut.

She went home; whether immediately or shortly after her death is unknown. In the beginning, they weren't even sure that it was her, as the early events were dismissed as natural phenomena, a creaky old house, wind, or imagi-nation. After all, some odd sounds are to be expected when moving into an old house. But it wasn't her time to die, and in death no one came to meet her[1], to guide her to where she was supposed to be. So, she did what came naturally: she went home, back to the place that she knew and loved. But as if death hadn't been traumatic enough, she arrived to find everything had changed. Her mother was gone, having been evicted. All the furniture, all things familiar — including even her personal belongings — had been removed. Only the house remained. She wandered the cold dark house as a lost soul. She was waiting, for what else could she do? She played through her short life's accumulated memories to keep her company, to attempt to find the answers to the dilemma that she now faced.

Soon the strangers came moving in, taking over the house. Her house. Her room. They didn't seem to pose a threat, and she eventually took comfort in Kellie's company, whom she regarded as a loving, caring mother figure.

chapter 3

It wouldn't be hard to believe if you were there. If you were to strip away the satellite dishes and modern automobiles, and situate yourself in the old courtyard, you could be standing in any era in the history of this grand estate, for very little has changed. Yet late at night, when the fog claws its way up the shoreline, consuming the lakefront community, the hands of time spin backwards to a bygone era. If you stand quietly in the gardens you will see the shadows of the deceased move around you to the beat of their own drummers.

You remain still, afraid to breathe for fear they may take notice. You then realize for a brief moment, while hiding there in the dark, that being alone with them makes them the reality, and you the ghost. Your eyes quickly dart from doorways, to pathways, to windows in the hope of finding someone — anyone — living, which will validate your reality.

At the turn of the nineteenth century, a wealthy family built the mansion on a sprawling lakefront property, turning their vacation property into a permanent residence. The owners were extremely active within the community and the church, opening their home to social clubs and society parties, as well as helping to establish and build one of the area's first libraries. In the 1920s, the mansion changed hands, having been purchased by a self-made millionaire named George who had immigrated to Canada from Europe.

He moved in with his wife and daughter. As his business grew, so did the estate. A bowling alley, indoor swimming pool with saunas, and a variety of other houses for family and servants were added. The landscape was transformed by beautiful gardens and fountains; several underground tunnels were also built. A long time confidant was placed in charge of the small army of servants that now lived permanently on the property.

Though his duties were those of a head butler, he considered himself more of a foreman. He was honoured by being granted two small rooms as his personal living space within the mansion, which meant that he didn't have to bunk with the rest of the help in the outbuildings.

The young daughter was cherished by her father, who enjoyed their time together when his business didn't consume all of his attention. The butler cunningly took the girl under his wing, becoming her friend and protector.

By 1939 the war in Europe was heating up, and Canada joined the Allies in the effort. In June of 1940, Italy declared war on the Allies, and the RCMP began to scrutinize the owner of the mansion. They investigated George primarily because he was a well-to-do immigrant who owned several large Canadian companies. Another point that made the RCMP take notice, though, was the fact that their subject had direct ties to Mussolini, with whom he had even exchanged gifts. By the end of 1940, the owner of the property was arrested for complicity and sent to an internment camp in Northern Ontario. The government took control of the estate, while the wife and daughter moved to their other home outside the province. The head butler was left in charge of the property, the remaining servants, and the operating budget.

With his newly appointed position of power and the absence of the family of the estate, his true self emerged; he ruled the workers in a way that would have made any dictator proud. The staff quickly learned to be loyal and obedient.[2]

chapter 4

*Incessant running in the hall above my head; whether
is it being chased and is fearful or it has a playful nature, I
do not know. I do know that I am supposed to be alone in
this house.*

Over the next few weeks, sounds of walking on the stairs, running
in the upstairs hall, and loud crashing became more frequent. These
noises were unnerving for the occupants, as well as for friends and relatives who would stop by to visit. Guests at the house would normally feel that a presence was watching them with disapproving eyes, and
most described a pressure pushing down on them, as if they were
submerged in deep water. No one had a reasonable explanation for
these occurrences.

Kellie felt as if she were being followed throughout the house, and
more often than not, she was followed by distinct footfalls and creaking
floors. She felt that there was some type of bond being established. This

was becoming more and more clear, at least to the women, as these activities always occurred in proximity to them.

One day, they heard walking in the living room. The sound entered the kitchen where they sat, and stopped near the table. Then, directly behind Kellie, a tapping on a pane of glass in a cabinet further announced that they were not alone. This closeness disappeared as the men arrived in the house. The noises continued, but they were now happening on a different floor. Actions like this demonstrated that whoever was making the noises had little fear of the women, but disliked being around men.

Al worked with a lot of the people who stopped by to visit. He wasn't about to hint about ghosts, as he was concerned about sounding crazy to them. He was struggling with the idea himself, looking for any other possibility. He decided that they had to know what was going on. Something had to be done. He borrowed a microcassette recorder from his employer and purchased a new tape and batteries for it. He then gave Kellie instructions about what to do when leaving the house the following morning.

Al left for work earlier than usual the next day. Shelby arrived at the house and met Kellie to go out shopping. Before they left, Kellie closed all the windows and turned off the television. She retrieved the recorder and set it on the mid-stair landing, depressing the record button. As they left the house she signaled their departure by calling out, "Good-bye, we're leaving now," as the door was slammed shut. The house was vacant and securely locked.

Immediately following the door being shut, the recorder taped footsteps coming down the stairs and the thump of bare feet landing heavily on the main floor. Mixed in with these noises is the jingling of what sounds like charm bracelets. Next comes a heart-wrenching sigh of despair, as if all hope is lost and this person has been completely abandoned. A neighbourhood child singing outside can be heard in the background. Almost immediately, there is running on the stairs, a slight microphone distortion as a hand picks up the tape machine, and a distraught voice asking, "Mother, why?" before the machine is turned off with a click.

Later that day, the recorder was found where it had been left; only two minutes of the thirty-minute tape had been used. As the recording was reviewed over and over again, there was a mix of feelings and emotions. First, there was a sigh of relief as suspicions were confirmed that something was going on in the house and everyone was assured that they weren't going crazy. Then came the realization that there was something unseen roaming their home. What if that horribly despairing sigh had been from the girl who used to live there? Excitement from the confirmation quickly turned to sadness.

chapter 5

*Running; always running down the hall to the bath-
room, knocking on the bathroom door.*

One morning, Kellie noticed that the perfume bottles on her dresser
had been moved. She had been sure of their original arrangement, and she
mentioned it to Al and I. We arranged them again and noted the specific
location of each bottle. This would make it easy for us to detect any tam-
pering with them. When we checked them soon after, we discovered that
they had been moved again.

Occasionally, Al and Kellie would go downstairs in the morning and
discover that either the front or the back door had been unlocked. It
seemed that the girl's spirit was able to interact with physical objects, so
maybe it was possible to establish communication with her. We discussed
various methods that we could employ in our attempt. We opted to start
with the most direct method: we would speak to her and use the tape
recorder, as she had already demonstrated her ability to use this device.

Al and I went upstairs to the master bedroom. The house was silent that day. Al set the tape to record and I spoke, calling her by name — which we had learned from the neighbours — and assuring her that we meant her no harm. Then I said that if there was anything that we could do to help her, or if she had anything to say, to please use the tape recorder. After that had been said we waited a few minutes, then went downstairs and waited in the kitchen. When the allotted thirty minutes were up, we returned to the master bedroom and retrieved the tape. We reviewed it, and found that aside from an odd repeated tapping noise midway through the tape,[3] there was nothing.

The next day Al and I arrived at his house and entered through the back door, into the kitchen; we must have surprised her, as there was a distinct shuffling on the hardwood floor in the living room a few feet from where we stood. She seemed to retreat in the presence of men, which was quite understandable given what my preliminary investigation had revealed about her experience with them. However, she never demonstrated fear with the women in the house; in fact she seemed to take comfort in their presence. The girl formed a closeness with Kellie; she seemed to need a motherly attachment that was safe and loving.

In retrospect, perhaps communication could have been established if it had been initiated by Kellie, as the girl's fear of men may have kept her silent that day. We continued to tape every chance that we could.

One afternoon, a girl arrived at the front door and explained that she was a friend of the girl who had lived in the house previously. She insisted that she needed to see the girl's old bedroom. She was very polite, and the nervous conviction in her voice persuaded Al to allow her to enter the house and go up to the girl's old room by herself. He waited at the bottom of the stairs with the girl's mother. A few moments later, the girl came down crying and left.

> *Girl screaming*
> *"Oh my God!" (Girl)*

Crying
"Close the door." (Man)
"I'm not your little girl!" (Girl)
Excerpt from surveillance tape

A candle was found that had been removed from its holder and placed across the room under the radiator. Once discovered, it was replaced in its holder. The next day the same candle was pulled from the holder and thrown into the same spot as it had previously been found, this time with a resounding crash as it hit the floor. We that felt this could be some type of communication, and that the spirits were trying to tell us something. The area was scrutinized to no avail, and the episode's meaning remained a mystery.

We noticed that events in the house had started to change. They were now more often than not being announced prior to occurring — a loud crash in the corner of the master bedroom was usually a precursor to running being heard throughout the house, for example. Other times, there would be roaming smells like that of burnt toast, burning wood, and rotten eggs. Also, pictures on the wall and lampshades would all be found tilted in one direction in the morning.

We also found that some of the mirrors in the house would be coated and smudged with a powdery white substance, enough to cover large portions of them. The exact composition of this substance remains unknown.

The events were becoming annoying and unnerving to Al and Kellie; Hailey, on the other hand, still seemed to be oblivious to the activities, and that was how they wanted to keep it.

It was a beautiful Saturday morning; the sun was bright and warm, and there was a slight breeze coming off the lake. Al woke to the sound of someone shuffling around the dresser. He turned to see a woman with short hair wearing nothing but a towel, searching for something to put on. He closed his eyes and went back to sleep, assuming that it was simply Kellie. He rose about an hour later to discover his girlfriend at the kitchen table reading the newspaper, still wearing her bedclothes from the night before. He asked her if she had been at the dresser that morning, but she said that she hadn't.

Later that day, when I arrived at the house, he told me about this sighting and the mystery grew even deeper. We knew what the girl looked like (from pictures that Al's neighbours had shown us) and the person that he had seen wasn't her. So who was it? We had to find out. We decided then and there that we should investigate the long history of the house and its property.

The first thing we were going to do was continue with the audio taping, and introduce a video recorder as well. In discussing these recordings, we agreed that the house would have to be as controlled an environment as we could possibly make it. This meant that all electronic equipment was to be shut off prior to taping, all windows and external doors were to be closed, and no one at all was to be in the house. The problem was that we could not pinpoint any one specific location in the house to focus our investigation on, as the incidents seemed to be running rampant throughout. It was decided that sections of the house would be investigated in a systematic pattern.

Baby powder was spread in a four-by-four-foot square, overlapping the threshold of the master bedroom. This section of the floor was sealed off, and we waited. Upon examination of the powder several hours later, a crisp, clear boot print was found. However, no one in the house owned a pair of boots with treads like this, and no one had been allowed to go upstairs. From information that I had gathered, we knew that the girl who used to reside in the house wore boots like this from time to time.

chapter 6

Someone enters
"Hello, Marty, Michael, Mommy, Martin?" (Girl's
voice calling out)
Whispered conversation
Two girls giggling. One a child, one older.
Excerpt from surveillance tape

Later in the year, the four of us went to a party at a friend's house. As we mingled, we were introduced to a guest at the party who told us that he used to live next door to Al and Kellie's house (this would have been the middle portion of the former servants' residence). We got to speaking and he told us that when he lived there in the mid-seventies, the place had given him the creeps. He remembered one instance in particular in which he saw a woman in one of the bedrooms who simply vanished when he approached her. The interesting thing was that his description of her matched what Al had seen that morning so many months ago. To be seen in both places could possibly mean that she had lived in the house when it was one large dormer, when all of the attaching doors were still in use. It could also possibly lead us to her identity.

We discussed this turn of events. The investigation was starting to get complicated. We knew that the young girl was there, and now it seemed that we had another resident there as well. It was going to be difficult to distinguish which spirit was causing which phenomena. I wondered if the two spirits had met in the house, and what their reaction to each other was.

Kellie was vacuuming the upstairs hallway; she had just made her way to the master bedroom when the vacuum shut off. She checked the switch, then noticed that the plug had come out of the wall at the other end of the hall. She put the hose down and started to walk toward the plug. It lay on the floor in a coil of excess electrical cord. It was obvious to her that she had not accidentally pulled the plug out of the outlet. As she reached for the cord, she heard a creak from the stairs. She froze, her eyes fixed on the top of the stairway. She waited a moment, then moved to the landing and peered around the corner with her breath caught in her throat. Kellie was seized by terror, as just ahead of her on the stairs was a solid black figure.

She could make out the head and shoulders, and a body that went straight down and stood on the stair; however, its body was devoid of all features. She couldn't scream, as her chest was constricted with fear; she wouldn't scream, for it would know she was within its reach. It seemed to be moving away from her — drifting away slowly, down toward the main floor.

As she retreated back up to the second floor, back to the master bedroom, she realized that her only escape route was blocked; she was trapped, and she knew that it didn't matter how solid the bedroom door was, it wouldn't stop this type of intruder from reaching her if it wanted to. She scrambled for the phone, placed an emergency call to Al, and told him to get home right away. He arrived a few moments later. Finding the door locked, he let himself in and called to her. She called back from the bedroom. He searched the main floor, then worked his way up to her. No one was found, and nothing was out of place. They both went downstairs and sat at the kitchen table until her nerves calmed.

We set up audio surveillance in the living room. We ensured that all electrical equipment was off, that all doors and windows were closed, and that everyone would leave the house for the hour that we needed to complete the taping. Al and I waited outside.

When the hour was up, we entered the house from the back door and stood silently for a few minutes in the kitchen. A slight noise came from the second floor, but nothing further.

Al retrieved the tape recorder and we went back outside to review the tape. There seemed to be nothing on it, then right at the end of the tape came a conversation between two females; one of the girls called out two names as the tape ended. Al recognized the voices and the names, but wanted verification. He led me to a neighbor's house and asked him to listen to the tape. After hearing the tape he asked were we had gotten it, and we explained that it had just been recorded. He showed disbelief and told us that the voices were those of the deceased girl and her mother (still living), and that the two names being called were their pets'.

We discussed the theory of residual haunting and the possibility that memory events were somehow imprinted within the house and being triggered by something we didn't understand.[4] How else could we explain the mother's voice being recorded on the tape when we knew that she was still alive? The problem now was that if this theory was correct, then how did it explain the incidents in the house with the rocking chair and tape recording equipment? At this point we had no idea.

Several of the tenants within the mansion were complaining of noises, missing items, and seeing strange things in their apartments. One tenant even went to the property manager to complain about his digital alarm clock going off at five-thirty each morning, regardless of the time it was set for. It would go off even when it wasn't set at all. He reported that he had tried different electrical outlets, and had eventually gotten rid of that clock and purchased a new one. The same thing occurred. He asked the property manager to check the wiring and fuse box in his apartment, which was done. Nothing was found to be wrong.

Other tenants reported their alarm clocks going off at the same time. I was about to dismiss these events as neighborhood power outages, when

I heard about another person in the building who had the same trouble, the difference being that his alarm clock was battery operated.

chapter 7

Jon was a good friend of mine who, as a psychic, had a great interest in the paranormal. Al and I spoke to him about the events that we were experiencing in the house. He happened to reside in the old mansion, and already knew about some of the problems. We let him see our photographs and listen to our tapes, and he couldn't believe that we had collected so much in such a short time. He had a computer lab that was capable of enhancing the tapes, and offered to try to remove some of the static from the recordings. This was a break for us, as we knew that there was valuable information in some of those indiscernible whispers of conversation being hidden under layers of static.

We discussed the events that were taking place in the mansion with Jon; he told us about tenants in various apartments in the grand old house who spoke about strange noises, heavy breathing emanating from empty rooms, things going missing, and some type of problem that the tenant in the basement was having. Another observation he had was that he had never seen a relationship between couples who moved in last very long. Regardless of how long they had been together prior to moving in, or how happy or in love they were, they all quickly broke down with fits of rage and severe arguments. One couple who were very much in love moved in, and within a week they were fighting and throwing each other's belongings off their balcony into the driveway. Jon went outside and found the male walking around in circles and asked if he was all right. He seemed confused, and said that he didn't understand what had happened between him and his wife, since they had been happy together for the last seven years. This happened to every couple that moved into the mansion. Married or not, all relationships quickly failed.

Hailey woke up at around three-thirty in the morning. She was thirsty, so she climbed out of bed and went downstairs to get some apple juice. As she got to the bottom of the stairs and turned the corner into the living room, she froze. Her eyes fell on a solid black figure walking from the fridge to the dining table. Her fear pushed her back upstairs and into her bedroom. For some reason that she couldn't explain, she didn't wake her mother or Al, she just sat in her room and cried.

Al woke to the sound of her crying and went to check on her. She told him what had happened downstairs. He told her that it was okay, and that he needed a drink as well, so they should both go down and get something to drink. They went downstairs and into the kitchen. Nothing was there. Hailey told him that the figure was about as tall as Al (5'8"), solid black, with no discernable features like hair, or a face, or anything else, but that she still somehow knew that it was a man. They drank their juice, and then returned to bed without further incident. Soon after this event though, Hailey went to stay with a friend for a few weeks.

This was becoming more and more complicated; we knew that the girl had come back to the house because of our tape recordings, but who was this dark figure that had been seen twice? If it was a man, where did he come from? And, more importantly, what did he want?

> *"Come here! I'll get you!*
> *I'll get you!"*
> *Excerpt from audio surveillance tape.*

It was a beautiful Saturday afternoon. Al informed me of a noted increase in activity in the house. We decided to go out for the day to get away from the place, so Shelby, Kellie, Al, and I piled into the car and left.

We returned that evening around six o'clock and were about to settle in at the kitchen table for a game of cards when we heard someone on the stairs heading up to the second floor, then running down the hall to the master bedroom. This was followed by two loud crashes. Al and I went up to investigate. Each room was searched, but no one was found and nothing was out of place. We returned to the kitchen and the noise started up again. The four of us sat and listened to the banging, crashing, and running above our heads. The activity was the most intense that any of us had yet heard.

Al wanted to set up the camcorder, and I agreed. As we prepared to go upstairs and discussed the best location to set up, Kellie and Shelby moved into the living room. We set up the tape recorder on a cabinet in the living room, close to the bottom of the stairs, and Al pressed the record button. We then cautiously climbed the stairs, armed with an instant camera. We stopped abruptly mid-way up. Just ahead of us we could hear a shuffling in the hall, first retreating, then heading back toward the master bedroom. We also wanted to retreat, but we continued up. I snapped a picture as I stepped into the bedroom, but there was nothing there.

As I set up the video recorder, Al took the instant camera and tried to aim it in several directions at once. The video camera was set up in a position to view the doorway and the entire hall, which included the middle bedroom door, the bathroom, and the bend in the hall that leads to the stairs. We returned down the hall, chased by uneasy feelings, descended the stairs, and joined the girls in the living room.

As we returned, Kellie told us that there had been walking in the kitchen. Shelby described high-pitched noises; two separate but indistinguishable sounds coming from the front of the house, between the living room and the main floor bathroom. She expressed it as being like the sound that a light bulb makes just before it burns out. She said that the noises occurred as Al and I arrived on the upper floor. Al retrieved the tape recorder from the cabinet and played the tape. We heard ourselves going up the stairs and the girls talking in the background. We then heard the noises that Shelby had described. These sounds obliterated all others on the tape. Then, as if a hand had been placed over the microphone, nothing but muffled sounds could be heard until our descent on the stairs. At this point, the recording returns to normal, documenting us coming down the stairs and the girls talking in the living room.

The four of us sat and listened to what seemed to be an army on maneuvers upstairs. We waited there for an hour, then Al and I went up to retrieve the videotape. As we proceeded up the stairs we could feel the energy: the atmosphere became thick and heavy, almost crushing. It was like trying to walk under water. We reached the camcorder and found that it had been shut off. When I ejected the tape and looked at it, I estimated that fifteen minutes of tape had been used. We started back down the hall; Al was approximately six or seven feet ahead of me, recording with the tape deck as we went. I was suddenly struck by a cold wind that went right through me and ripped the air from my lungs. It passed quickly, and as it did, my eyes started watering for some reason that remains unknown to me. I felt a flood of emotions that I knew weren't my own; I was engulfed by fear, desperation, and confusion — but mostly fear. Then came the icy pins and needles, as if my entire body had just awoken and the blood had just started to flow through my veins. I stopped in my tracks, as I had become momentarily disoriented. I couldn't get my eyes to stop watering. Al had slipped around the corner, making his way to the stairs. He noticed that I was no longer following him, so he turned around and came back for me. He looked at me standing there and asked me what the problem was. I didn't want to discuss it there. I just wanted to get away from that spot.

Once again he took the lead, but this time I followed very closely. We made our way down the stairs and joined Kellie and Shelby in the living room. We explained what had happened upstairs, and they told us that after we had gone up, they had heard someone go up the stairs behind us.

As we further discussed what had occurred upstairs, Al rewound the tapes. We reviewed the videotape, which clearly showed our backs as we walked down the hall after setting it up. A few minutes into the tape a tapping started on the microphone, then the camera was shut off, and the picture went to snow. On reviewing the audiotape, we heard our movements and our conversations in the hallway, just as we had expected. When it got to the point where Al returned and he asked what the problem was though, a male's voice, almost overlapping Al's, said "Come here," followed by a sinister "I'll get you!"

We shut the tape off and the room grew quiet and ominous. It was now painfully obvious that this male spirit was pursuing the girl.

We played through the tape again, revealing a second "I'll get you," but little more. I thought about the feeling of fear that I had experienced upstairs, and I knew that my fear was for her, trapped in this house and being pursued. What were his intentions? From the sound of his voice on the tape, they were anything but good. We would have to help this girl. But how?

Just then, a pounding on the stairs brought my heart to a pause, and the four of us exchanged fearful glances. Extremely heavy footfalls, slow and deliberate, were coming down the stairs. Whatever this thing was, it was mad — possibly because we had interrupted its pursuit of the girl. Now it seemed that we were about to find out what its intentions were. A loud banging on the front screen door made us all jump in terror. It was Kalena, the girl from next door. Her arrival had interrupted whatever was coming down the stairs. We let her in and asked her if she had seen anything on the stairs, as she would have been able to see the lower stairs from where she had been standing. She said that she hadn't, and joined us in the living room.

She asked if she could see the video, so Al put it on for her to watch. Just as it ended and went to snow, the closet door right next to the couch flew open with great force, slamming into the wall. We all jumped again. Kalena leapt up and left the house immediately. We felt that we had little option at that point but to follow suit, so the four of us abandoned the house as well. As we were about to leave, Al retrieved a bible from his bookshelf and put it on a cabinet — an action he could not explain, as he was not a devout Catholic. He placed the audiotapes on the book as we left. That night they slept at my apartment, and in the morning Kellie told me that Al had searched my bookshelves, found my bible, and slept with it next to him all night.

We ventured back into the house the next morning. The main floor was quiet and still, but when we went upstairs we found evidence of a struggle. I felt a sickening gnawing in the pit of my stomach. Starting at the top of the stairs we saw dark black heel marks on the white tile floor, as if someone had been pulled or dragged. The marks continued down the hall, around the corner, and into the middle bedroom. They proceeded unhindered under furniture, as if it didn't exist. We also found a smudged handprint on the corner of the wall where the hall turns. The direction of the smudge was consistent with someone trying to stop themselves from being dragged.

Had the girl been caught by this other spirit? If so, what had happened to her? I felt a twinge of guilt for leaving the house the previous night. If we had stayed, this might not have happened. We went to review the tapes, but they were all blank. This was strange, as we had listened to them the previous night and there had been a great deal of information on them. The strangest thing of all was that the tapes remained blank for several days, then the audio returned, and we found that the information had not been lost. This event remains a mystery to this day.

> "... off ... get off me!" (Girl screaming)
> Excerpt from audio surveillance tape.

In the days that followed that Saturday night, the atmosphere in the house was different. It felt sinister. The activity was no longer random noises, but rather specifically focussed to annoy us at inopportune times. It seemed clear that if the menacing spirit did indeed control the girl now, his next plan was to force us out in an attempt to have full control over the dwelling.

Over the next few days, the spirits began to play games with us. We were still unclear at this point exactly how many spirits we were dealing with, but we suspected that it was three of them.

It started one morning when Al and Kellie got out of bed and went downstairs, only to find that the garbage bag had been shredded and its contents strewn about the kitchen. Things also began to go missing; a new package of razor blades, a twenty-dollar bill, keys, and a half a bag of donuts were among the casualties. The bag was eventually found, with three donuts still in it, stuffed into the coffee maker on a shelf in the kitchen.

Shelby and I arrived at the house to visit, and the four of us sat around the kitchen table. Hailey was still staying at a girlfriend's house. We decided to play a board game, so Kellie put some water on to make tea and Shelby went to the living room closet to retrieve the game. She opened the closet door and reached up to the top shelf. As she did so, an unseen force grabbed her hand and pulled her into the closet. A girlish laugh followed, and the temperature in the closet plummeted. She pulled away with great difficulty and hurried back to the kitchen. I went directly to the closet, but aside from the extreme cold I found nothing. I couldn't account for the temperature, however, as no part of the closet touched an exterior wall, it was adjacent to a large radiator, and the hot water pipes that fed the house ran through the back of it. If anything, the closet should have been warmer than the rest of the house, and usually was, except for this particular instance.

It took us a while to talk Shelby into staying, but she finally agreed. When we began playing the board game, my wife jumped. I asked what the problem was, and she stated that something was touching her hair. We watched, and sure enough the hair at the back of her head was being moved by some unknown means. We got up, put our shoes on, and left the house.

The next morning, Al and Kellie were in their bedroom folding and putting away laundry. On the nightstand, a crucifix that had been given to Al by his mother stood just behind a clock radio, as it had for many months. The crucifix held special meaning for Al, as it had been used in the religious service at his father's burial. That evening, the crucifix leapt from the night table and flew across the room at them from approximately seven feet away, landing at their feet. As it hit the floor, all the nails popped out and the image of Christ separated from the cross. Al exploded in a mix of fear, frustration, and anger. He directed an onslaught toward the dark spirit, issuing ultimatums and threats, at which point all went quiet.

chapter 8

Our investigation would entail hundreds of hours of research into the history of the property, its structures, past owners, and subsequent tenants, staff, and servants. Searches of municipal, provincial, and federal archives were conducted; miles of newspaper microfiche were studied; assistance from the local newspaper research department was enlisted; and a trip to the Police Museum was made. All provided small clues to this perplexing puzzle, as well as presenting some bizarre circumstances. For example, a gentleman who worked at the Police Museum knew one of the property's previous owners quite well, and assured me that nothing out of the ordinary had occurred at the estate during the man's time there, which, according to newspaper articles that we researched, couldn't be further from the truth.

Something was missing. I needed to find the piece of the puzzle that told me why this male spirit was here. I knew that there had to be a reason why he remained. He seemed to have established a very powerful base — not only in the old servant's quarters, but also within the old mansion itself. There was something that tied him to this place, and it wouldn't let him leave.

Al and I inspected the property, searched the tunnels, and looked at the buildings from top to bottom. The old file room, where dozens of old wooden crates full of dusty yellow paper had sat untouched for years, was also checked. At the sight of these boxes, I just stood there wondering where to start. I was starting to lose all hope, and the task that lay ahead seemed futile. Defeated, I looked at Al and told him we'd come back another day. As I turned toward the door to leave, though, for some reason I glanced down at a crate that was sitting on top of an old cabinet. A corner of a piece of paper stuck out no more than a half an inch out of the rest of the files. I pulled this paper out and looked at it. I read it again. I couldn't believe what I was reading, so I handed it to Al for confirmation. It was a letter from a tenant who had lived in the house that was now Al's. Not just any tenant, but the first tenant to inhabit the house after the property was sold.

The letter was a complaint. The tenant had only been in the house for one month and was already giving his notice to move out. The reason stated in his letter was that there were noises in the house. As nothing could be done about these noises, the letter continued, he had no option but to move. Over the following three weeks, the rest of the files were searched, but other than this letter, nothing related to the investigation was found. It was as if this paper was practically handed to me just as I was on the verge of giving up. At the time it was hard for me to believe. It became easier over time though, as I started to see how things worked.

The house that Al was living in offered its own mystery. It was a large structure that had no basement, which was not a mystery in itself as there are many old structures that don't have basements. However, every other structure on the property did have a basement — even buildings that wouldn't normally have one, such as the garage. There was also an array of subterranean passages. It was apparent that the man who had owned the property in the 1920s had a passion for expansion, which he had demonstrated both above and below ground. So why did the second largest structure on the property not have a basement? Could this be part of the mystery? We were determined to find out.

An article that I read about the property led me to its author, a local historian, who pointed me in a few directions. These yielded other small bits of information, but still nothing that would truly assist in solving the mystery of this dark figure.

One cool, sunny Saturday afternoon, Al and I were in our garages, busy with woodworking projects, as we normally were on weekends like this. Neighbours and passersby alike would stop in to chat, or to see what was being built. As a gentleman in his forties was passing by, he noticed Al, and stopped to say hello. They exchanged greetings, and I introduced myself. Al mentioned that the man had lived in the house in the early 1980s. We stood in the street looking at the house. During the conversation, Al asked him if he had ever had any problems in the house. The man was quick to respond, "No, not really." Then he added, "The odd difficulty with the plumbing." A broad smile crossed his face, indicating that he might have more to say.

Al prodded, "No other problems?"

He nervously shifted his weight. "Well, my father used to sleep in the small room at the front," he stated, pointing up to indicate the top-floor bedroom. "He would complain of something bothering him during the night. Whatever it was would pull the sheets off of him, and sometimes tickle his toes." I noticed that the smile had vanished; he now looked quite serious.

"What did you do?" I asked.

He laughed. "We moved out!"

The conversation moved on to other things, and the man soon continued on his way.

Al and I stood there on the road looking up at the house. Leaves fell around us, fluttering in tiny swirls, only to be carried off on the breeze. We could feel the crispness in the air and knew that winter was riding in on the wind's long tail. It was the time of year when people put away their barbecues and lawn furniture and retreated indoors. For those who lived in this house it was an ominous prospect.

A friend of mine referred me to a lady who ran a spiritual church. I had heard of this lady, as one of my relatives had met with her about twenty years before and had been astounded by her ability. My friend relayed to the woman that I was particularly concerned for the safety of the girl's spirit. She agreed that a rescue was necessary, but added that it would be several weeks before we could meet, as she was not well and was staying in the hospital. Finally though, a date was set and I informed Al and Kellie.

She arrived at the house around noon on the agreed date, with two other ladies as a support team. They entered and introduced themselves to Al and Kellie. As they spoke, she wandered the main floor for a few minutes before rejoining them. Al gave her a picture of the girl that his neighbour had given him. She ran her hands over it, then turned to Al and asked that a kitchen chair be brought into the living room. He retrieved the chair and placed it in the middle of the room, so that she sat facing the couch. The rest of the group sat on the couch and, after a few minutes, joined hands and prayed for protection.

The room was silent as the woman concentrated and moved into a trance-like state. She called the girl by name, asking her to come near. The lady stated that the girl was hesitant because there was someone else there. She again asked the girl to come to her, and she finally came forward, kneeling at the woman's side. The lady stroked her hair, and told her how beautiful she was. Then they spoke about many things, her love of dogs and horses, for example, and other things that she couldn't possibly have known about the girl. She told her that staying in the house was not a good thing. The girl replied that she couldn't move on because of the suicide, and the lady explained that that wasn't the way it worked. The girl cried that she hadn't meant it, and that it had been an accident. She stroked the girl's hair to comfort her.

Then the dark spirit came forward and stood just off of the bathroom, trying to tempt the girl back to him. Though we couldn't see the spirit itself, we did see shadows moving around the bathroom door. The lady half turned and asked him to leave, but he refused. They both became angry and an argument followed that had both of them shouting and swearing, though we couldn't hear the spirit's voice. Realizing that the argument was getting her nowhere, the lady stopped and told him, "You've made your own hell, so go rot in it." With that, he left the house. She then turned to the girl and told her that he had been teaching her bad things. "You have to go on to where you are supposed to be." The girl then left, and went on her way.

She came out of the trance and asked for a glass of water. They all got up and went into the kitchen. She told Al and Kellie that the girl wouldn't be back, but that this other one, the male, had only left temporarily. Not only would he be back, but he would probably be there forever.

Before they left, Al offered a donation to her church, but she refused. The three women said their good-byes and went on their way.

A week later, Kellie sent a thank-you card and a cheque to the church, wishing to donate something. The cheque was returned to them, voided.

chapter 9

Over the next four weeks or so, it became apparent that this spirit had the power to do many incredible things, one of which was the ability to mimic any one of us. He began doing it often, playing games with us by duplicating our voices exactly.

Kellie was in the bath the first time that it happened. She heard Al desperately calling to her from the bottom of the stairs. She yelled back that she was in the bath, but the calling continued until she got out of the tub and went to see what he wanted. She wondered what could be so important. She was quite surprised to find that she was alone in the house, with all the doors locked. She phoned Al at work, and found that he'd been there the whole time.

Another time, Kellie was upstairs with Hailey, helping her find something, while Shelby was downstairs waiting for them at the kitchen table. They both heard the other call them to the stairs, and both went to the staircase to find out what the other wanted, only to learn that neither of them had called out.

Another strange phenomenon, which was noted on two occasions, was bright flashes of light going off, identical to a camera flash. The first time it occurred was as Kellie entered the master bedroom to check on Hailey, who was watching television. As she entered, the room lit up with a brilliant flash of light, startling them both. The second time was on Christmas morning as the two of them came into the living room together.

I believe that these flashes were reproductions of the countless flashes that had been endured by the spirit in our quest to photograph it, as mimicking seems not only important to it, but also easy for it to use to its advantage.

Kellie was babysitting for a friend on a temporary basis, and had put the child down for a nap. She felt tired herself, so she lay on the couch and drifted off. A short time later she heard someone come in the back door. A voice asked her, "Are you all right?" She recognized the voice as Al's. Still groggy, she half opened her eyes and saw him cross the living room and go upstairs. She got up and followed, but when she got to the second floor she found that other than the undisturbed sleeping child she was alone in the house.

Kellie was on the main floor cleaning the house; she saw that it was approaching noon, so she stepped out the back door to speak to her daughter. It was a beautiful summer day, and Hailey was outside playing with a friend. Kellie announced that she was going to make lunch, and Hailey asked if her friend could stay. Kellie said that would be fine.

The children decided to go upstairs to play with Hailey's dolls as they waited for lunch. Kellie went to the kitchen to prepare the meal, as sunbeams pushed through the windowpanes. The house seemed bright and airy, but something darker was emerging upstairs.

The girls sat on the floor in the middle of Hailey's bedroom playing with several Barbie dolls. They were her favourite toys, and she was proud to show them off to her friend. As they played, something began to happen near the far bedroom wall. In a pile of toys on the floor there was a slight movement, then the Ken doll became animated, stood up, and began walking over to where the girls sat playing.

Kellie was laying out lunch on the kitchen table and was about to call the girls down when she was startled by frantic screams and running on the stairs. Fearing that one of them had been hurt, she ran toward the stairs. The girls flew around the corner, almost running into her. In their panic, they tried to explain what had happened, but it all came out in a jumble. She had to let them calm down before they could tell her what had occurred. They told Kellie that they had snatched up the Ken doll, tied him in a plastic bag, tossed him into the bedroom closet, and locked the door. They then went into the kitchen and ate lunch quietly, after which they refused to go back upstairs. Kellie wasn't about to go up to investigate — she would leave that up to Al when he returned from work. When her friend went home, Hailey decided to play downstairs and out-side for the rest of the day.

Al worked with a woman named Susan who was looking for a babysitter. He mentioned it to Kellie, who met with Susan to discuss details and arrangements. Kellie agreed to watch Susan's two-year-old son at home.

They came over and brought a basket of toys, a playpen, and a high-chair, among other items. The visit went well, and a sitting schedule was discussed. Kellie started watching the child the following week, and for a while everything went well.

One afternoon when Kellie went upstairs to wake the child from his nap, she found that he was already awake in his playpen, playing with his toys. She was sure that she hadn't left any toys with him while he slept. The next day he had fallen asleep downstairs, so she carried him upstairs to the front bedroom and put him in his playpen. She made sure that there were no toys in with him this time. When she went up to get him later, how-ever, he had his toys again.

A few days after that, the child was overtired and cranky, so she put him in his playpen with a bottle of juice and read to him until he fell asleep. Once he was sleeping, she put away the book and placed his bot-tle on the dresser. Later on she discovered that he had his bottle in the playpen with him, though she had put it well out of his reach. That night she mentioned the incidents to Al, who came home with a baby moni-tor a few days later. He set it up so that Kellie could hear the child from anywhere in the house as long as she kept the mobile receiver near her. Several days passed without incident.

One afternoon Kellie heard someone walking on the second floor above her; she also heard it on the monitor. The child started to make noises, then a man's voice came over the monitor, saying "Shhh, be quiet," and calling the child by name. The child responded "Bye, bye. Love you!" Then the person walked away, heading toward the master bedroom. She called Al at work and told him to come home right away, then went up to get the child, who seemed fine. No one else was found in the house.

Another day, Kellie was in the kitchen on the phone with the boy close by in his highchair, placing coloured plastic rings on a peg. He dropped one on the floor, and Kellie couldn't reach it. When she hung up the phone, she looked for the ring, but it wasn't where it had fallen. Then she noticed that he had it in his hands.

Later that week, Al and Kellie were sitting on the floor in the living room playing with the child, waiting for his mother to arrive for him. They amused him with a puzzle made out of padded plastic animals. The puzzle was nearly completed when they discovered that the bear piece was missing. They were sure that all of the pieces had been there when they sat down to play with the boy. Al found the piece standing on its side near the closet door. He went over to get it, and as he reached for it, it fell over. They told Shelby and I about the incident when we arrived later that night. The four of us tried to get the bear to stand up, but as it had rounded feet and a protruding seam running around its entire edge, it was impossible for us to do.

We decided to set up a camcorder in the bedroom, switching it on when the child went to sleep one day. We watched the video after the child went home. It showed the child waking up and starting to cry, but nothing else. The audio portion, however, revealed a man's voice going "Pssssst!" which woke him. Then the voice made noises similar to those that a pig would make. These noises terrified the child.

Kellie brought the playpen down to the living room and the child slept there from then on. A few days later there was activity upstairs, sounds of someone walking around and banging. The child became agitated; he went to the bottom of the stairs and said "Al, upstairs." He kept repeating this, then became frightened and started to cry.

Susan got off work early one day and went to pick up her son. She realized the time and knew that Kellie had gone to pick Hailey up at school and had taken the boy with her. She let herself in the back door, went into the living room and sat on the couch to await their return. As she sat there, she heard walking upstairs going into the bathroom. She assumed that Al was home early from work. She heard the water turn on and off, and then the toilet being flushed. She went to the front door and looked up the street to see if Kellie and the kids were on their way back. When she saw Al walking down the street toward the house, she went out and told him about the sounds she had heard from the second floor. He went into the house and upstairs to check, but it seemed that she had been alone in the house.

Also heard on occasion was a child's voice calling "Mommy" from the top of the stairs. This only happened when there were no children in the house.

chapter 10

The butler was a loyal worker who had served the owners well. As a reward, he was placed in charge of managing the property and the staff. Because of the family's social standing, it wasn't acceptable for them to worry about menial tasks. They had more important things to attend to, such as running the family business and entertaining important people, so the care of the property was entrusted to him. He accepted the job with open arms, and his sense of self-importance grew.

He started believing that he was something more than he really was. He shed his old work clothing and began wearing sharp black suits. This was a symbol of his power and domination that would command respect from the staff. He felt somehow entrenched in the hierarchy of the family, later feeling that he was a part of the family unit itself. He was a force to be reckoned with, but he was quickly and secretly learning to despise the owners every time they questioned him or second-guessed his decisions, especially when his orders were overturned in front of the staff.

His personality was that of a cruel and sadistic tyrant who feared physical confrontations with men unless he had the upper hand, and who took his frustrations out on women, children, and defenceless animals. He considered himself a ladies' man, but was actually a pervert who would force himself on the female staff members; and when they spurned him, he would retaliate with fits of rage or by making up false claims against them to the owners of the property, resulting in disciplinary action or dismissal. Few challenged him. The women would try to avoid him, and feared being alone with him. They would try to work in pairs; however, living on the property, this wasn't always possible. He had a habit of walking in on them in their private quarters — even when they were in the bathroom.

He worked closely with a woman whose job it was to maintain the mansion. One afternoon, the woman's brother arrived from the United States. He needed a place to stay for a while. He traveled light — a simple suitcase and a well-worn doctor's bag. He moved into the servants' quarters, sharing his sister's living area. He professed to be a doctor from the U.S. traveling abroad on vacation; the truth was that he had fled the States because he was being sought after by the authorities for questioning in the performance of several unlawful medical procedures. He felt that Canada was much safer, at least until the heat was off and he could return home.

He was a smooth-talking, well-travelled professional, who was quickly accepted by the property owner and his family. Although they were leaving for some time to stay at their other residence, he was welcomed to stay there for as long as he wished. Due to his acceptance by the family, he immediately fell under the suspicious eye of the butler. The doctor sensed this and he, in turn, watched the butler. He felt that there was something that he liked about the man, something that reminded him of himself. Was it the subtle playful hints that he despised the authority of his masters? Or was it the way he showed contempt for those below him, especially women? This was the beginning of a match made in hell.

One evening, they found themselves alone in the courtyard enjoying a cigar. They spoke of the world, its trials and tribulations, and how hard things were in these war-torn years. Then the doctor, for some reason, decided to take the butler into his confidence. It was at this point that he divulged that he was an abortionist. In the days that followed they became friends, and soon forged an alliance, their goal being to make as much money as they possibly could. The butler would provide a safe place for the doctor to ply his trade, as well as find girls in need of his services. They would split the money.

chapter 11

He walks through the house with an unchecked authority.

Over time, Kellie became the main focus of the malevolent spirit's attention. It was unclear exactly why, but it could have been because of the fear that the spirit evoked in her; or maybe it was simply in its nature to dominate and terrorize women, children and small animals, as it had during its life. There were a few occasions in which it attempted to frighten the men in the house, but he had little success, as our desire to investigate pushed aside our fears and we pursued him in every possible way. As for Hailey, she would tune out and virtually ignore its activity altogether. This left only Kellie to face the games that he played.

One morning as she was doing the dishes, she heard two distinct thumps in the living room. She turned her head to look into the room, but nothing seemed to be out of place. She turned back to the sink. The next moment, directly behind her, a man's voice screamed "Hey!" She turned around, startled, but no one was there.

A couple of days later, she got into a warm, relaxing shower after breakfast. There was a noise outside the bathroom door, which she strained to hear over the flowing water. Without warning, the shower curtain flew open, and she was gripped in the icy clutches of terror. Even though she couldn't see anything in the room with her, she knew that something was there. She felt exposed and vulnerable, so she leapt for a towel and quickly wrapped it around herself as she rushed out into the hall and toward the bedroom. Everything sitting on the back of the toilet tank flew off — untouched — and crashed to the floor.

Shower-related incidents happened several times. On occasion, the curtain would be pushed in on her. One time, the water kept adjusting itself to hot, and she had to keep readjusting it to avoid being scalded; she received two slaps to the back of her head, which forced her into an immediate retreat from the shower.

It was the middle of the night when Al slipped quietly out of bed, trying not to wake Kellie as he crossed the room and went down the hall to the bathroom. On his way back to the bedroom as he passed the open doorway of the playroom, an unseen entity tempted him to look into the room with a loud "Pssssst!" He ignored it and went back to bed. The next day he told me about the incident, and stated that he wished he had had his camera with him at the time. Who knows what it might have captured? I felt that there was something sinister about the event, and told him that maybe it was a good thing he had ignored it.

On another occasion, Al got up around three o'clock in the morning and went into the bathroom. While he was there he began to feel strange; a dizziness washed over him and caused him to break out in a cold sweat. The room began growing dark around the edges. Al would later describe the sensation as being like tunnel vision. He tried to return to his bedroom, but his legs had become sluggish. On his way down the hall he passed an antique loveseat, which he collapsed over. When he awoke, still feeling dizzy and weak, the better part of an hour had passed. He made his way back to bed, and noticed that he had sustained an injury to his abdomen in the fall. When he awoke later that morning he felt fine, though the bruise on his stomach remained for several days.

Later that Fall, I was sitting on the couch with Al. He got up and went into the main floor washroom. I soon heard laughter coming out of the washroom. It was definitely a male, but it wasn't Al. Then I heard Al start to laugh — a mocking laugh. He then swore, telling the other voice where to go, and its laughing stopped. When Al returned to the living room, he told me that the laughing had come from the hallway outside the washroom.

On several occasions, Al heard voices outside his bedroom door. Once, after Kellie had fallen asleep, he heard whispers in the hall. He strained to hear what they were saying, but he couldn't make it out.

Another time he awoke early, and Kellie was still sleeping soundly. He lay there debating whether he should get out of bed, when from the bedroom door he heard a woman's voice whisper, "They're still sleeping."

One night they were up late, lying in bed talking, when a male's voice stated "Go to bed," as if they were disturbing him.

Eventually, the stressful nature of this situation started to wear on Al, and he began to show contempt for the spirit. He started taunting it by swearing and shouting at it, and although the hauntings continued, events stopped occurring around him. Furthermore, if his arrival interrupted an incident, it would stop, and the spirit would retreat.

There were retaliation attempts made by the spirit. On one occasion, for example, the couple found their bed to be soaked. However, the water had been dumped on it in such a way that only Al's side of the bed was wet.

Al and Kellie took in a small dog, as its owner was moving and had to give it up. They welcomed her into their home, and thought that she would be a good companion for Hailey. All went well for a short time. One night, however, the dog was crying to be let out of the master bedroom, where she usually slept. When she was let out, she ran down the hall, bypassed Hailey's room, and entered the little room at the front of the house. Once she was there, she began to whine and cry. When she was called back, she started down the hall toward the master bedroom, but then she appeared to be confused, as though she were caught in a tug-of-war. She stopped in the middle of the hall and turned in circles, unsure whether she should go to her calling master or return to the little room. Finally, she made a choice and went back to the little room, and Al had to go and get her. This happened several nights in a row, then stopped for no apparent reason.

One day, the dog charged out of the kitchen as if someone had pinched her on her hindquarters, and was chasing her through the house. Then came a crash from the empty kitchen. When the noise was investigated, it was discovered that her food and water dishes, along with their contents, had been thrown against the cupboard. This occurred a second time when the dog lay on a small rug in front of the kitchen sink. The rug was violently pulled, upsetting the dog and startling her into a frantic retreat from the area. Again, her food and water bowls were slammed into the wall. This time, though, Kellie was sitting at the table and witnessed the incident.

> *A white figure moved from the stairs to the bathroom.*
> *"It had no feet!" Ann exclaimed.*

It was approaching one o'clock in the morning, and Ann, Kellie, Shelby and I were sitting around the kitchen table discussing the various activities that had taken place in the house. Al and Hailey were already in bed. Ann, a relative of Al's who had come to visit for the weekend and was staying in the house, had witnessed a tube of lip balm being thrown from the nightstand in the bedroom earlier that evening. As we talked, I noticed something in my peripheral vision. It was the figure of a person off to my left in the living room, who was apparently listening to our conversation. The being appeared to be composed of black smoke or mist, and as I turned to get a better look at it, it retreated with terrific speed to the living room closet. Ann had caught a glimpse of it as well and said that it was a dark shadow that had stood in the open doorway between the kitchen and the living room. She said that it had been standing where the couch was located, but that the couch didn't seem to affect it at all. It simply stood there as if the couch didn't exist.

The conversation dwindled after the encounter, and it was now close to daybreak. Shelby and I decided that we had better head home, so we said our good-byes and left the house. Ann went upstairs and prepared for bed. She was spending the night in Hailey's room, and just as she got into bed and lay down to sleep, she heard a man's voice whisper "Good night" into her ear. She said good night back and went to sleep.

It was nearly two-thirty in the morning when neighbors and friends started to take their leave of a small party at the house about a week later. Several of us stayed around to help clean up the chip bowls and stack the lawn chairs.

When everything was done, Al and Kellie lingered outside a few minutes longer to enjoy the breeze that was coming up from the lake. They finally went inside. Kellie headed upstairs while Al made a final check of the main floor; he locked all the doors and turned off all the lights before he, too, made his way up to bed.

The temperature upstairs was borderline unbearable, so Al decided to open the window in the front bedroom to catch any available cross-breeze. Kellie climbed into bed as Al struggled with the window. Something caught her eye. An ominous black shadow that was the size and shape of a man moved next to the master bedroom closet, and glided along the wall toward the bedroom door. As it went out into the hall, she jumped from the bed and called out to Al, warning him that something was coming in his direction. Al went out into the hall, but he saw nothing. She described what she had seen, and told him that she felt like it was still upstairs somewhere. He asked her to go downstairs and retrieve the camera. While she was gone he heard whispering, but it was coming from no specific direction; it seemed to be everywhere at the same time. He could not make out exactly what the whispers were saying, but he clearly heard his name mentioned several times. He stood his ground.

Kellie came back up with the camera, and they began their search of the upper floor, looking for anything that was out of the ordinary. As they moved away from the stairs, the smoke detector activated downstairs. They called off the search, since they had to go down to find out why the alarm was sounding.

They found nothing wrong on the main floor. The detector was in working order and had a fresh battery. They didn't find any reason for it to have gone off, and once it was reset, it remained silent. They quickly went back upstairs and continued their search, but nothing was found, so they went to bed. The rest of the night was uneventful.

chapter 12

Al heard noises above his head again as he sat in the kitchen. They started as they usually did, with a loud crash in the corner of the master bedroom. He retrieved his instant camera and crept up the stairs. A sound came from his bedroom, and he rushed in and snapped a picture. He scanned the room as he stood in the doorway. Everything seemed to be as it should. When he checked the photo, he noticed a light or glare around the nightstand mirror. He took the picture down to the kitchen to study it more closely, and at that point he noticed the images in the mirror. It struck him as being odd that this was the corner where the loud crashes always announced the beginning of the spirits' visits.

He called me at home to tell me what had happened. I rushed over to examine the picture. It was the most incredible one that I had ever seen. It seemed to contain the three people that I felt we were investigating. It appeared that something was being played out in this image that might be an important event to them, or that might provide us with clues to this mystery. The man in black stood facing away from us, his hands clasped behind his back. At his side stood a curly-haired girl holding a doll, looking up at the man. Just outside of the room was a woman wearing a puffy-shouldered waistcoat, turning on the stairs to run up them.

We went up to the master bedroom and took several control photos from where Al had taken the original picture. The only thins that were captured the in mirror were Al's legs, part of the floor, and the bed.

A few days later, I spoke to Al about trying a simple experiment. As it occurred to us that each incident was announced by a crash in the corner of the master bedroom, and it seemed that the mirror had something to do with these incidents, I wanted to see if we could stop these events — or at least alter them. We securely placed a black cover over the mirror, and went downstairs to wait. For what, I wasn't sure.

It wasn't long before a crash came from the corner of his room. We were about to rush upstairs to investigate, when it began to sound like someone was destroying the room. We slowly made our way upstairs. Nothing seemed out of the ordinary, and the sounds had stopped by the time we arrived. However, the noises that we had heard made it seem to me that the spirits were extremely upset about the cover over the mirror. Al decided to leave the cover on for a few days. I told him that if this mirror were some type of a doorway, it would only stand to reason that they would be upset about the cover. The problem was that we didn't know if they were trying to get in, or if they were already in the house and the mirror was a way for them to get out.

After spending several hours studying the photo of the mirror, Al and I had found a few clues that led us back to the mansion. It appeared that the image showed the foyer, the stairway, and the doorway to the old library. We decided to go directly to the mansion to compare the photo to the actual layout. I felt that this was a good opportunity to take some readings of the house, so I grabbed some of my equipment and we walked over to the main entrance. As we entered, I turned on my gauss meter to get an electromagnetic field (EMF) reading.

We stood looking over the photo. It was evident that whatever significant event had been captured in this image had occurred here, at this spot in the house, as the lines of the door to the library, the railing, and the stairs matched exactly. We started to discuss the importance of this photo, when the meter signaled something on the stairs. Al readied the instant camera. As we moved closer to the staircase, a white Siamese cat darted past us, giving us a start. We breathed a short sigh of relief just before the meter activated again. Something else was there, moving away from us up the stairs.

We pursued the signal upward and paused on the top landing, as the signal was growing stronger. It then diminished as whatever it was continued to move away from us. We followed it down the hall, around a sharp corner, and down another hall, stopping outside a locked room next to a servants' stairway that led back down to the main floor. The signal stopped, then disappeared. We then realized that we were outside the former butler's quarters.

I scanned the area, but got no reading. Whatever we had been chasing seemed to be gone. We stood there for a few moments, and then a creak behind us led me to scan the hallway from which we had just come. I regained the signal and we gave pursuit, but this time as we arrived at the turn in the hallway, the signal simply vanished. We searched for another twenty minutes to no avail, then we headed back to Al's house.

A strange complaint was circulating through the property management office, and around the complex, from a couple living in the basement of the mansion who were reporting ghosts in their unit. We approached the couple prior to them moving out, and the male tenant granted us an interview. His girlfriend didn't stay for it because she was on her way to work. He invited us into his apartment and took us on a short tour, which ended in the living room/bedroom. I asked him what had happened. He looked to the floor and stated that weird things were going on: noises, sounds, and personal belongings being moved or going missing. I asked if these occurrences were so frequent that they were enough to force him out of his apartment. He told us that a couple of weeks before, he and his girlfriend were awoken between two and two-thirty a.m. by a noise. They were confronted by a tall black figure standing at the foot of their bed, who suddenly just vanished. I asked if it could have been a dream. He said that he wished it were, but that they had both seen the same thing at the same time. He told us that they didn't sleep for two nights afterward. That's when they decided to move out.

I asked him where the figure had appeared, and he took us to the area where the edge of the pullout couch would come and pointed to the spot. We couldn't help but notice that the section of floor that he indicated was sinking into the ground. It was about four feet by four feet around, and sloped down to a depth of about a half an inch in the centre. We inspected the floor and looked around the apartment for a few more minutes, then thanked him for his time. Outside, Al and I discussed the significance that the sinking floor might have, and the possibility that the dark figure could be the same figure seen in his house. If so, this link could lead us to its identity. Al said that he would arrange it so that as soon as they moved out we would get access to the unit.

My friend Jon introduced me to Mrs. Jones, who lives on the main floor of the mansion where the picture in the mirror seems to be focused. She mentioned that there had been some strange incidents occurring in her unit, so I asked for an interview and she agreed. During the interview she told me about personal items that had gone missing and of the occasional sound of breathing in the rear sunroom. Whenever this breathing was investigated, it would stop.

Mrs. Jones had held a family and friends get-together in May. Several of the guests reported that something unseen had brushed past or touched them. One woman was grabbed on the shoulder; another, who spent the night there, left the next morning and refuses to return to the house. Unfortunately, she will not say what happened. The most interesting incidents Mrs. Jones told me about involved a solid black figure that she had seen twice. The first time, she was in the sunroom when the dog started barking at the back door. She looked up, and through the French door she saw the shadow looking in at her. She said that she could not make out any details, but for some reason she felt that it was a male. She reached down to calm the dog, and when she looked up again, the image had vanished.

The second incident occurred at approximately three o'clock in the morning. She awoke to find a solid black figure standing at the end of her bed. She said the thing was blacker than the darkness of the room. She reached for the light, but when she turned back, it was gone.

At the conclusion of the interview she stated that she was going to purchase a Ouija board, but I advised against this. She wanted to find out more about what was going on in her home, so I told her that if she wanted information she should contact a professional institution and have them send a tested psychic. She agreed, but I haven't spoken with her since, so I don't know if she ever followed up on it.

chapter 13

The spirits hated the fact that we had been investigating their activities over the past two years. We utilized an arsenal of electronic equipment in an attempt to monitor not only the environment and how they were affecting it, but also to try to catch their images in a photo or on video. As much as they disliked our overt intrusions as we tried to see into their world though, they loved the undivided attention that it afforded them. It was noted that as our investigation intensified, the phenomena escalated. Our interest was apparently matched by theirs.

When summer came, we stopped for vacation. The events dropped off sharply. Even after returning to the house afterwards, it seemed overly quiet, so we held off on using our cameras and other equipment.

In the manner of a child crying out for attention, small events started to occur, as if they were trying to entice us into resuming our investigation. I was interested to see how far they would go. We kept the cameras at the ready and refrained from using any other electronic systems. I was going out on a limb. I wanted to see if reverse psychology would work, so we planned to openly show disinterest toward their activities.

Small occurrences started almost immediately. Kellie was in the kitchen, alone in the house, when three small pebbles materialized out of thin air and startled her when they landed on the corner of the counter by the sink. Their origin was unknown, and they got her attention. Next, an old, graying, rotting material bandage showed up in the upstairs bathroom. Hailey was disgusted when she found it; she said that it reeked of decay. It, too, seemed to have come out of thin air. The third time was when Kellie was in the kitchen again, preparing something to eat. She stood by the microwave oven next to the fridge, when the freezer door opened by itself. This time Al was home, so she called to him and he was ready. He ran into the kitchen, snapping a picture from his camera in the general direction of the commotion. The picture came out and showed a light/energy distortion spiraling upwards from the fridge to the kitchen ceiling. We decided to recommence the electronic portion of our investigation.

We had set up a mini security surveillance camera, which was easy to conceal in the master bedroom. The camera was hidden in some clothing and angled toward the door; it viewed the hallway and the bathroom at the end of the corridor. Thirty minutes later, when we had finished taping, we went upstairs to review the tape. It seemed that we were going to have difficulty in reviewing it, however, as the camera became plagued with technical problems. First it wouldn't rewind the tape, then it wouldn't play it back. This equipment had been used and tested prior to the taping with no trouble at all. We contacted a man who had a great deal of experience with this equipment to have him take a look and give us an opinion as to what was wrong. He checked all the devices and found them to be functioning properly, except for the fact that we couldn't get them to play back. We brought in another television and hooked the recorder up to it, but the problem persisted. Then something finally happened. As we were trying to view the tape, the entire picture on the screen was pulled to the side of the television's frame of view, as if a very powerful magnet was being drawn across the screen of the TV. There was no reasonable explanation for this occurrence. When we were finally able to view the tape, we found that it contained nothing. The equipment was sent back to the owner, who tested it and found that it worked perfectly.

Will they give up their closely guarded secrets of the past?

We entered the deep recesses of the mansion, moving cautiously, deliberately, as if we expected an armed attack. The smell of mould and mildew assailed us, the atmosphere was heavy, and there was a weighty feeling of dread. I felt something else: the awakening of a long dormant instinct, lost to our evolution and a life in civilized society, but it was fully awake now, telling me "don't go in there." A ripple of fear rode a wave of adrenaline up my spine to my brain. I wasn't alone in this feeling, for I saw the same dread in Al's eyes as he reached for the door handle.

"Ready?" he asked me as he gripped the doorknob.

I moved into position like a commando about to storm a stronghold. Raising my camera, I signalled to him and he pulled the door open. We were momentarily blinded as I fired a shot, the flash bleaching out our night vision.

We forged on into the room, our flashlights chasing shadows; there was a spike on the gauss meter, signalled by a buzzing, then nothing. There it was, the sinking section of the floor, and the only section of this massive basement that was not poured concrete. Al pointed to the radiator. Its pipes headed down into the floor. It was the only radiator in the basement where the pipes didn't go back up to the main floor. This indicated the possibility that there was a room below.

"This is where they saw it," he said, indicating the area near the fireplace. The previous tenants had slept in this room. One night they had both been awoken by a noise, and both had seen a solid black figure standing at the foot of their bed. Before they could react, it had vanished. This event had been followed by uneasy feelings until they moved out. We inspected the area, getting down on our hands and knees. There was a slightly raised section, which caused an indent in the tiles. It was approximately four feet by four feet. We wondered if this might be a hatchway. This area was plywood, while the rest of the floor was older hardwood.

Al set the tape recorder on the mantle of the fireplace and pressed the record button. As we retreated to the far room, he pushed the servants' buzzer, long since disconnected, then closed the heavy oak door behind us as we left the area. He knocked at the door a few times, and we stood there half expecting an answer. None came. We continued investigating the adjacent rooms. One of the rooms was the old wine cellar, which was built like a vault; its floor, walls, and ceiling were all poured concrete. The walls were sheathed with steel, and at its entrance were two solid steel doors. The outer one was equipped with a heavy locking system. This door was opened to reveal a second door, which opened inward. It felt more like a jail than a wine cellar. We decided that it was time to go, as the tape would have finished recording by then; we went to the oak door, and as Al pulled it open, I snapped another photograph. We did a final inspection of the room, retrieved our tape recorder, and left.

Later, we inspected the photos. What we saw in the second photo was disturbing. There, lying before the fireplace, was what appeared to be the skeletal remains of a person — an image that did not appear in the first photo. We had to go back immediately. A control photo was taken from almost the same location and angle as that of the subject photo. Nothing unusual showed up in this picture; however, upon comparison of both photos, one can see the pattern on the rug, and in each photo these patterns are identical throughout. The only difference is the image in that first picture.

We began to review the tape recording, hoping for further clues.

We listened to the tape, straining through the static and white noise. "There — what was that?" I asked; I thought I'd heard a voice in the static. Al rewound it. What was it saying? He rewound it again, then it became clear and turned our blood cold: "Let me out, let me out, let me out!"

Now we had a voice pleading to be let out, which seemed to correspond directly with the photo of what appeared to be bones, all from the same room, one made directly after the other. Could this be the mystery? What if it was? What if this truly indicated a body being buried in the basement of this grand old house? We now had to face many new problems and questions that weighed heavily on our consciences. Morally and legally we felt compelled to do something, to report this. But to whom?

The police would laugh us right into an asylum; the current owners would be more interested in why we were snooping around the basement; and the other, more pressing problem was that, if for argument's sake, this was an unsolved murder and the individual or individuals who had done this were still alive themselves, they might do anything to maintain their secret. We had a great deal to think about.

Kitchen, 2:30 p.m.: Just after the freezer door moved by itself, a white mist appeared near the ceiling.

Kitchen, 7:25 a.m.: A noise in the room prompted this photo; note the images on the closet door.

Bedroom, 4:30 p.m.: This is the photo that led us to the old mansion; close inspection of the mirror shows a dark male figure, a woman on the stairs, and a child holding a doll.

Living Room, 12:15 p.m.: This Easter photo shows a man looking in the front window; notice the illumination which seems to come from outside. The straps of his tank top are highly visible.

Tunnel, 11:55 p.m.: We could not find any source for these lights.

Basement, 9:05 p.m.: The image of a skeleton on the floor, the legs near the door, the skull closer to the fireplace.

chapter 14

A pendulum is an instrument that can pick up energy and relay answers to specific questions by way of turning clockwise, counter-clockwise, swinging back and forth, or pointing. It can be any small object that hangs plumb on a string, chain, or wire. It is an ancient device that even has references in the Bible, such as Jacob's Rod[5].

Pendulums have also been used by professionals such as mineralogists, archaeologists, and the British and U.S. militaries for intelligence gathering, as well as by police forces to locate bodies.

During our taping sessions, in which Jon interviewed the spirits, the pendulum would indicate responses to specific questions. In an attempt to understand and verify the pendulum's responses, I used a sound meter and audio recording equipment to try to capture any response by way of electronic voice phenomena (EVP). We had great success with our recordings, capturing specific responses to direct questions; each EVP was indicated by activity on the sound meter, and each meter indication corresponded to recordings of voice or sound not heard by us at the time of taping. There were also slightly elevated meter readings, which corresponded to sounds and voices responding to questions that were both heard by us and captured on the tape. It was further noted that by directly furnishing Jon with false information on which to base his questions, we would receive the correct information in reply to his questions. Some of these replies showed frustration and anger, which in my opinion demonstrated intelligence and emotion.

When we entered the vacant house, we went directly to what used to be the middle portion of the servant's quarters. Jon, Al and myself stood in the kitchen for several minutes, feeling out the house. We then toured the main floor, finally venturing up to the second floor. The house was dark and silent. We examined the rooms, closets, and old doors that used to pass through to Al's side. Jon picked the central room to ask his questions in. We settled into the room, setting up our tape recorders and sitting on the floor. Jon prepared himself, and was going to use a pendulum to try to receive yes and no answers to specific questions. We waited for a few minutes for Jon to get comfortable, then he began.

Q: Is there a spirit here who wishes to communicate with us?
A: No.

Q: Is there a spirit present in this house?
A: Yes.

Q: Does this spirit, or any other spirit, wish to communicate with us now?
A: No.

Q: We are all friends here, no one wishes to hurt you, and we wish to help, so there is nothing to be afraid of. We want you to know that if you have anything to say, or if there is anything we can do to help you . . . is there anything we can do to help you?
A: No.

Q: Is there anyone present at this time, amongst the three of us, that should leave? That the energies would have leave?
A: Strong no.

Q: We are all friends here; no one wishes to harm anyone. Are you afraid?
No answer.

Q: Do you wish to harm us?
A: No.

Q: Were there beatings that took place in this house many years ago?
No answer.

We stopped the question period, as there was too much outside inter-ference from other spirits. The spirits were deliberately playing games with us. We couldn't believe anything that we'd heard to that point; noth-ing was credible.

We sat in the dark room waiting for Jon, who was busy trying to refo-cus on the pendulum. He began again,

Q: Are there spirits in this house?
A: Yes.

Q: Do they move between here and the house next door?
A: Yes.

Q: Were the spirits here witness to many beatings?
A: Strong yes.

Q: Did anyone die from these beatings?
A: Yes.

Q: Are they buried on the property?
A: No.

Q: Did these deceased spirits come back here?
A: Yes.

Q: Were they murdered by one person?
A: No.

Q: Were people killed in this house?
A: No.

Q: Was this year 1941?
A: No.

Q: When these deaths took place, was it in the decade of the 1940s?
A: Yes.

Q: Was it between 1940 and 1945?
A: No.

Q: Was it between 1945 and 1950?
A: Yes.

Q: Was it 1946?
A: Yes.

Q: Was it in the year 1946 that a murder took place in this house?
A: Yes.

Q: Was somebody arrested for this crime?
   No answer.

Q: Was somebody arrested for this crime?
A: No.

Q: Was the person who was murdered a child?
A: No.

Q: Was the person who was murdered a woman?
A: Yes.

Q: Did she have short black hair?
A: Strong yes.

Q: Was the name of the person who committed this crime Edward?
Pendulum stopped mid-swing; no movement.

Q: Was the person who committed this crime named Edward?
Jon told us that the spirit refused to answer out of fear.

Q: Does Edward show himself as a black figure?
A: Weak no. Great fear.

Q: Don't be afraid. Are you afraid now, of someone here?
A: Yes.

Q: Are you a child? Are you a ch...
A: Yes.

Q: Do you like to hide in kitchen cupboards?
A: Yes.

Q: Are you a little girl?
A: Yes.

Q: Do you like to play with dolls?
Heavy shake along the plumb line of the pendulum; fear; no answer.

Q: Do you like to play with children?
Fear; no answer.

We quit the question period, and decided to leave the tape machines to continue recording as we left the house.

Later, we re-entered the house to retrieve our equipment. The atmosphere in the house was overly oppressive and heavy; all three of us experienced our ears popping. We wandered the main floor. The longer we remained in the house, the hotter it seemed to get. It was becoming extremely hard to breathe for all of us. We went upstairs to get the tape and stopped at the top of the stairs. At the end of the hall near the front bedroom we heard a sigh, followed by a stifled a whimper that became a sob. We went to the room and found nothing. We collected our equipment, and I started to snap pictures, trying to capture a tiny fleeting blue light, which eluded my camera.

The tapes were reviewed over the next couple of days. There was a great deal of whispering conversation, but one thing seemed very clear: a male's voice asking, "Did you give them my name?" There were also slapping sounds and sounds of crying on these tapes.

chapter 15

The spirits of the dark haired woman and the little girl still resided in the house that in their lives provided them with shelter, remaining behind for reasons known only to them. They continued to interact with the living, trying desperately to participate in the happy times that the occupants enjoyed. Maybe it brought them satisfaction and pleasure to feel that they were a part of the lives that they remained so close to; perhaps these happy events even allowed them to feel alive again. Times of happiness, joy, and even sadness usually triggered a memory response from these spirits, causing an escalation in paranormal activity. These two seemed trapped, but I am unsure as to why. They may have remained in the house for their own reasons, or possibly continued on there by design. There must have been times when they faced their own torment, their own hell, as they watched the living share times of joy and happiness, and then faced a flurry of their own personal negative emotions such as loneliness, and what must have seemed to them to be abandonment.

Also, from what our tapes have revealed, they were constantly the victims of this dark figure. He returned to them, and the terror he instilled was ever present. He seems to have had full control over their existence. Unless this cycle is broken, he will forever victimize them, and they, in turn, will always remind him of his crimes against humanity, constantly showing him what he has become, and virtually condemning him to his own private hell.

Our time in the middle unit had come to an end, as new tenants prepared to move in, totally unsuspecting of what they may encounter there. But we gave our word that we would not tell them anything about what was going on. We could only hope that if an event occurred, they would mention it to their neighbour.

It was noted as they moved in that the activity in Al's house increased. For example, as they took their furniture into the house, Hailey was in the upstairs washroom, and the door was pushed open. There was no one there. She came down and told us right away.

Jon came over to the house and met with Al, Kellie, Shelby and myself. The five of us sat around the kitchen table, discussing some of the current events in the house and our strategy on how we should proceed with the dig in the mansion's basement, should we get the authorization to go ahead.

Jon started to explain a theory regarding a loop linking the past with the present — how the past tries to repeat itself in the present by being influenced by an outside force. As he explained this theory, he drew a Lemniscate, a figure eight lying on its side (∞). This symbol represents eternity and regeneration; its endless shape also represents the balance of opposing forces.

He explained that this particular spirit used its energies to create occurrences, forcing us to repeat events that had occurred years before in his lifetime. This established a familiarity with him, and assisted in developing his power base. The whole time Jon was talking, he kept tracing this loop.

It was getting late and Jon was the first to leave. I reached over to pick up my can of pop, and as I did so my hand passed over the scrap of paper that Jon had drawn the loop on. I pulled it back immediately; it felt as if I had placed my hand over a burning candle. I looked at the paper expecting it to burst into flames. The others felt it, and all of them noticed the heat as well. There was nothing on, or around, the table that would have caused the paper to heat up as it did. The heat dissipated quickly.

Kellie excused herself from the table and went to the main floor washroom. A few moments later she rushed back to the kitchen, telling us of a black shadow that had crossed the washroom door. We went to investigate. The vestibule light was off, and the lamp in the washroom was on. We found no one and nothing out of place. As I moved around the small bathroom it occurred to me that, with the light on in the bathroom, and the light off in the vestibule, whatever it was that she had seen had to have been in the room with her, as a shadow or an image would not show through the windows of the door without some sort of backlight to cast a shadow. She wasn't impressed with my conclusion and commented that whatever it was, it really liked to hang around bathrooms.

That night Kellie could not sleep. Everyone else had gone to bed, but she remained downstairs reading. It was becoming early in the morning, and she decided she had better at least try to get some sleep. She went up to bed, being as quiet as possible so as not to disturb anyone. She climbed into bed and tried to find a comfortable spot, then lay there waiting for sleep to come. She suddenly felt something grip her leg at the ankle, then her other ankle was grabbed. Without warning, or time to react, her legs were pulled upward into the air, her head and shoulders crushing into the pillow and mattress. Panic set in and she tried to kick whatever it was off of her, but for some reason she didn't have the strength. A flailing arm tossed the covers aside as she reached for Al to save her. It was enough to wake him up, and as he did, the thing let her go. He switched on the light and she told him what happened as she scanned the room. There was nothing there.

chapter 16

"Let me out! Let me out!"
"So you're going to flip-flop!"
Excerpt from audio surveillance tape.

Jon, Al, and I entered the basement of the mansion. The authorization to tear up the floor had been passed down two days before, but this was the first common opening that the three of us had in our schedules. We settled in, laid our tools off to the side, examined the floor, and tried to decide on the best way to proceed.

Al started in the far corner by trying to pry up the floor panel. It fought him with every nail. This was going to be a long slow process.

Finally, the panel gave way and we pulled it free, placing it off to the side. What we were faced with was our first major obstacle. Under the wood was a poured slab of concrete, its thickness unknown.

We worked away, removing the wood floor and exposing the slab, looking for patchwork. None was found. What we did find were cuts in the slab that went right through to the earth below. This allowed us to see the thickness of the concrete, which was between one and one and a half inches. We took turns breaking the concrete along the fault line. This process was starting to draw out into hours. I looked at my watch and saw that we were running out of time, as the owner had been very specific: "No noise after dark."

We opened a hole that was two feet by two feet, and started to dig down. We encountered clay, which slowed us further. This was far more complicated than anything we had expected to find under the floor. The next major obstacle was encountered at a depth of one foot. Slate flagstones were found. We had to quit digging for the night. Jon produced his pendulum and stated that we should get some answers, as they may help us when we proceeded at another time. We decided to stop for awhile. We packed up the tools and went to Al's for dinner.

After dinner, Jon made up cue cards that read both A to Z and 0 to 10. We were going to try to get specific information this time, something that we could verify.

We returned to the basement and entered quietly, taking several photos and inspecting the site as we went. Nothing had changed, and nothing out of the ordinary showed up on the pictures.

We sat down on the floor. Jon would ask the questions, and I was to monitor the cue cards. The tape recorder was set to record and we started with our question-and-answer period.

Jon cleared the house of any threatening and negative energies, and requested that only truth be brought forth. He began,

Q: Is there a body buried in this basement?
A: Yes.

Q: Is the body buried in this basement that of a male?
A: No.

Q: Is the body buried in this basement that of a female?
A: Yes.

Q: Is the body buried where we have been digging? Are we digging in the right place?

A: Yes.

Q: Is it buried as it is shown in the picture?

A: Yes.

Q: Can you show us the location of this body?

A: Yes.

If I had had any skepticism, at this point it was gone, as I watched the pendulum defy physics and raise up, straining on its string thirty degrees, pointing to the location where we had been digging.

Q: How deep is the body buried in the soil — please answer in feet.

A: The pendulum pointed to the cue card with the number three on it.

Q: What was the year that this body was interred here, placed here?

A: 1.9.4.3. was pointed out on the cards.

Q: Was this person the victim of a murder?

A: Yes.

Q: Do you want us to find your body?

The pendulum went wild, turning as if attached to a motor.

A: Yes!

Q: Will you give us your name?

A: Yes.

We received the first name . . . Angela.

Q: We need your last name.

We received the last name . . . Carlucci.

Q: Was your full name Angela Carlucci?

A: Yes.

Q: Did you work here? Did you work here at your time of death?
A: Yes.

Q: Can you give us your age at the time of your death?
A: Yes.
1.9. was pointed at.

Q: Is your body the only body in this basement?
A: No.

Q: Is there more than one body other than yours in this basement?
A: No.

Q: There is your body and one more body as well?
A: Yes.
Jon paused to collect his thoughts.

Q: Were you pregnant at the time of your death?
Hesitation; fear.
A: Very weak no.

Q: We have to know the truth; were you pregnant at the time of your death?
A: Yes.

Q: Did this have something to do with your death?
A: Yes.

Q: Do you know the name of the father?
A: Yes.

Q: Are you willing to give us the name of the father?
A: Yes
We received the father's name . . . Joe Pacheco.

Q: Did the father of your baby have anything to do with your death?

Hesitation; fear.

A: Scared yes.

Q: Did he work here?
A: No.

Q: Who caused your death?
We received another name, a doctor's . . . Martin McCabe.

Q: How did you die? What caused your death?
A: Bleeding.

Q: Did you die in this house?
A: No.

Q: Did you die on this property?
A: Yes.

Q: After your death they brought you to this spot?
A: Yes.
Thank you!

We stopped for the night, packed up, and left the mansion. We stood outside discussing what we had received. It was up to me to try to verify some, or all, of this information.

The owner of the property stopped by Jon's house to check on our progress. Jon told him about the flagstone, which matched the stone around the fireplace, that we had dug out of the clay. He went silent for a few moments, and then he made the worst possible decision for our investigation. He told Jon that we had to stop what we were doing. We were to fill in the hole and not go back into this part of the house. We were shut down mere inches from verifying that there was actually a body buried there and exposing this long hidden crime and helping to put to rest this tormented soul.

When Jon told us, it came as a devastating blow; I was caught between ignoring the order and going down there to finish what I started, and just walking away. I felt sick.

chapter 17

The plan was going like clockwork. The butler had effectively spread the word, and the girls would show up — sometimes alone, sometimes with a male friend. The doctor would provide his service, occasionally assisted by his sister. The butler would have the fetuses incinerated in the main boiler, adjacent to the servants' quarters. With its sixty-foot smokestack, it resembled a crematorium. It seemed to be the best place to effectively dispose of the evidence of their business. This, of course, became a problem in the hot summer months, and another means to hide the evidence needed to be found; but, for the butler, the best part, aside from the money, was the absence of the owner and his family. This allowed them to continue their operation without being caught.

Then the unthinkable happened. A late-night knock at the mansion door brought a young man calling, looking for the doctor. The butler spoke with him briefly. He had seen him around and knew that he was seeing a young girl on his staff. He was furious, but business was business. He set the meeting so that all four could be present.

The next night they gathered in the servant's residence, the money was paid up-front, and the doctor performed the abortion as promised. This time, though, something went horribly wrong, and the girl started to bleed internally. The injury sustained during the procedure could not be corrected. They plied her with towels and the doctor sent his sister to fetch the butler from the main house.

When he arrived, he found the doctor distraught and fearful. The young man had fled, and the girl was bleeding to death. They stood there, watching the girl slowly die, trying to formulate a plan as to what they would do next.

The butler quickly came up with a plan. They took the girl to the mansion, under the cover of night, and carried her into the basement. They entered the games room, which was under renovation. Fuelled by adrenaline, the butler opened up the floor. Using a pick and shovel, he dug down through the clay to a depth of almost four feet. To even the doctor's horror, the butler tossed the nineteen-year-old girl into the hole. She moaned in pain as she landed on the cold damp ground. There was a brief argument. The doctor quickly backed down, as the man who stood before him was enraged, almost fanatical, and was holding the pick. The doctor knew that had the hole been slightly deeper, he would have been cast down as well. The butler lifted a heavy three-inch thick flagstone and dropped it into the hole onto the withering girl's head. This didn't seem to stop her from moving about, so he dropped a second flagstone on top of the first one. He then filled and packed the clay back into the hole.

He turned to the doctor standing in the corner. The doctor told him that it was too dangerous to continue, that it was over. The butler seemed to have calmed down; he just looked at the doctor and said, "You mean you're going to flip-flop."

The doctor simply nodded. Then he wasted little time; he packed and left that same night and headed back to America.

chapter 18

Not long after the digging stopped in the mansion, the hostile activity began to dissipate within Al and Kellie's residence. The child's activities continued, however; she would play with items that belonged to Kellie and steal the odd brownie.

I couldn't say that this investigation was over by any stretch of the imagination, but I could say that it had certainly been a complicated one — complicated by the multitude of spirits roaming the property. As I was sorting through their tragic stories and trying to understand why they were there, I began to understand that when one dies, there really isn't anywhere to go. All that have lived and died remained and continued to exist just slightly beyond our every day senses, overshadowing us. Their reality is timeless; they watch, interact with, and influence the living, while intermingling with other spirits.

The majority of spirits are silent. It's when they start to obsess over things they once knew in life that it becomes a problem for them and for the living people in close proximity to them, as they become bogged down in a thick underlying muck of emotions — hate, fear, despair, and broken dreams of what could have been. They are like us, equipped with 20/20 hindsight, and some wish that they could go back and do things differently, or change the past. They dwell on traumatic moments in their lives, punctuated with fleeting images of joy. Unfortunately, they become the tormented and the tormentors, by refusing to shed hurts, wants, and materialistic things, thereby progressing to a happier state of being.

It was late, and we had just arrived home from Al and Kellie's. We sat in the kitchen discussing a theory on communication, when something entered the room. The atmosphere changed, became thicker and colder all of a sudden. The energy came in intense swirls; anger and frustration seemed to be washing over us in waves. Our dog turned to leave the room and yelped, her rear falling to the floor as she ran for the balcony door. My wife grabbed the dog and retreated to the living room. The feelings of fear on my part, and anger radiating from whomever or whatever this was were so intense that my instincts led me to the sink, where I took the knives from the drip tray and put them into the drawer. I then joined my wife in the living room. She clicked the television on and turned the volume up loud. Several noises came from the kitchen, and the static hum and cold increased. My wife refused to look anywhere but directly at the TV, and the dog hid between us. The static hum continued for some time, finally dissipating, and the feelings that accompanied the sound were also gone. I don't know why, but I had the distinct feeling that I knew who this visitor was. I felt that it was the girl from the basement of the mansion. She wanted to be found so desperately, and the landlord had just completed repairs to the floor and was about rent the unit out again. I couldn't help but feel guilty, as if I had failed her.

We retired for the night, and all was quiet until two in the morning, when the intense hum returned in an attempt to get our attention. Upon failing to do so, it left our room, slamming the bedroom door behind it.

It was late morning, and the lady living in the basement of the house next door to the mansion was fed up with the noise coming from the apartment above her. She picked up the phone and called the management office to complain. Normally, the manager would explain that some noise is expected during the day; however, this call pushed him into immediate action. He contacted one of his staff, whom he told to meet him at the side door of the house. He grabbed the master keys from the lockbox and rushed to where his employee was waiting. He briefly relayed what the tenant in the basement had reported as they entered. The two men searched the unit but found nothing. The apartment had been vacant and un-rentable for some time.

We heard about this incident, so we went to speak to the tenant in the basement. She insisted that she had heard heavy walking and banging throughout the unit. After a short discussion, we decided that we had to get into the house to conduct further investigations.

A light snow was falling outside as we entered the house. It felt cold and empty. The three of us stumbled around in the dark, inspecting each room, guided by the single beam of my flashlight. We gathered in what was once a home office, with its rich oak-panelled walls, columns, and glass-doored bookshelves lining one wall. In one corner of the room was a hidden room, which, other than the wear, looked as it did over sixty years before, when it had been used as a wet bar. Jon lit a rather large cigar, saying it would create an ambiance. We moved to the front of the office, which was divided from the rear of the office by a wall to allow for a bedroom. Al took a position near the far window, Jon searched for a suitable location, and I set up my equipment in the center of the room and sat on the hardwood floor. Jon finally found his spot and settled down onto the floor as well, next to the door leading out to the hallway. Light chased shadows through the windows and across the wall, as the headlights from the odd passing car moved from the complex's parking lot.

Jon asked for protection against any threatening and negative energies, and requested that only truth be brought forth; then he began,

Q: Is this the house that George lived in?
A: Yes.

Mechanical failure of equipment, slight delay.

Q: Did George know of this girl Angela?
A: Yes.

Q: Was he involved with this girl?
A: No.

Q: Did George have anything to do with Angela's death?
A: No.
The pendulum stopped moving. Jon sensed a problem, a hesitation in the communication.

Q: Do you feel free to speak?
A: Yes.

Q: In the physical, were you a man?
A: No.

Q: In the physical, were you a woman?
A: Yes.

Q: Were you a resident here?
A: No.

Q: Were you a guest of the owner?
A: No.

Q: Were you on the staff?
A: Yes.

Q: Was your business in this house happy?
A: No.

Q: Can you give us the first initial of your name?
A: Yes.
The cue card with the letter E on it was pointed to.

Q: When did you reside here? The 1920s?
A: No.

Q: The 1930s?
A: Yes.

Q: Before 1935?
A: No.

Q: After 1935?
A: Yes.

Q: Were you born in Italy?
A: Yes.

Q: Were you happy here?
A: No.

Q: Were you harmed in the physical state?
A: Yes.

Q: Were you harmed by the owner?
A: No.

Q: Were you harmed by Edward?
   The pendulum stopped.
   Still.

Q: Were you harmed by Edward?
   No movement. After a few moments:
A: Yes.

Q: Is someone here now, threatening you? Scaring you?
A: Yes.

Q: Do you know a girl named Angela?

A: Yes.

A tremor occurred on the plumb line of the pendulum, indicating fear.

Q: Are you afraid of Edward?

A: Small yes, like a whisper.

Q: Did you die on this property?

A: No.

Q: Did you witness something very, very bad occur on this property?

A: Yes.

Q: Is it this unresolved guilt that keeps you here?

A: The pendulum swung in a wide arc, almost out of control, indicating yes.

Jon had to stop the pendulum to gain some composure.

Q: Was what happened your fault?

A: No.

Q: Is the guilt that you feel because you should have told someone about what happened?

A: Yes.

Q: Did this incident occur in 1943?

A: Hesitation, then yes.

Q: Have you been to the servants' residence?

A: Yes.

Q: Did bad things happen there?

A: Yes.

Q: Did abortions take place there?

A: Yes.

Q: Is this where you witnessed Angela being hurt?
A: Yes.

Q: Are you hiding here?
A: Yes.

Q: Are you hiding here from Edward?
The Pendulum stopped dead, as if it were anchored to the floor.

Q: Is the energy of the one we call Edward present?
A: Yes.

Q: Does he wish to speak?
A: Yes.

Q: Do you remain here because you feel you are still in charge of this property?
A: Yes.

Q: Are you still in charge of this property?
A: YES!

Q: Is there someone here you wish to harm?
A: No.

Q: Is there someone in spirit form you wish to harm, or keep under your control?
A: Yes.

Q: Do you harm them?
A: Yes.

Q: Is your name Edward?
No answer.
A long pause, still no response.

Jon said, "The same thing is happening tonight as it usually does; just as we start to get somewhere, this S.O.B. gets in the way and blocks us." We took a short rest.

Q: So, Edward, are you the only one here?
A: Yes.

Q: Are you afraid of being alone?
No answer.

Q: Are you afraid of being alone?
A: No.

Q: Are there others you keep behind you, so we can't speak to them?
A: Yes.

Q: Can we speak to them?
A: Yes.

Q: Is there anyone here who wishes to speak?
No answer.

Q: Is there anyone here who wishes to speak?
No answer.

We stopped our questions for the night, though the choice wasn't really ours to make. We set up new tapes to record in the bedroom and the bathroom, secured the doors, and retreated to the neighbourhood coffee shop to kill the half an hour that it would take for them to run their course.

chapter 19

The townhouse next to Al's was empty again. And so it went; people came and people left, and I had to wonder if they knew anything about what lived there with them. Did the forces here influence them? Al entered the empty house first, standing in the dark kitchen, the streetlight filtering in through the living room window, reaching like dead white fingers across the floor to where he stood. His body tensed as he heard the distinct sounds of someone rising off of a bed — the squeak of heavy springs and old fashioned metal strapping — in the room directly above the kitchen. He moved to the back door. He knew there was no bed; the house was devoid of all furniture with the exception of the fridge and stove. He stepped through the door into the cold night air to wait for us.

When Jon and I arrived, Al explained what he had just experienced. We entered the house and stood in the kitchen listening, but all was silent. I led them upstairs, looking in each room as we made our way to the front bedroom. We set up our equipment in silence. The heat in the room was stifling, so Al opened the window. Jon sat on the windowsill as I set up my tape recorder. I noticed that the door had closed behind us, so I asked Al to open it, which he did. It swung closed again. He opened it again, and again it swung closed. We laughed, and I said it was probably the way the door was hung. He opened it all the way to the wall and it closed again. I asked him if he could get it to stay at least halfway open, and as he reached for the door handle while it was swinging closed, it reversed direction and stopped at the halfway mark. He stepped back and I moved to look into the hall, expecting to see someone there. There was nothing.

We settled into the room and Jon began,

Q: We are present here as friends, and do not wish to harm anyone. Is there a spirit in this house who wishes to speak to us?
A: Yes.

Q: The one speaking to us, do you reside in this house?
A: Yes.

Q: Do you have intimate knowledge of the history of this property?
A: Yes.

Q: Are you free to share with us what you know?
A: Yes.

Q: Did a male worker named Edward work here in the 1940s?
A: Yes.

Q: Is there a body of a woman buried in the basement of the mansion?
A: Yes.

Q: Was she murdered?
A: Yes.

Q: I am putting a block of white light around this room; anything that is said here is only between us; no one can interfere with our conversation at this time. Do you understand?
A: Yes.

Q: The previous owners of this property, do they have anything to do with her death?

A: A weak yes, which may have indicated some knowledge of the incident, rather than direct involvement.

Q: Are you part of this?

A: No.

Q: Did Harry know of this murder? (Harry was a relative of George's.)

A: No.

Q: Did George know of this murder?

A: Yes.

Q: Was she pregnant at the time of her death?
No response.
He repeated the question.
Scared, no response.

Q: Do you still wish to speak with us? I remind you that you are among friends, and no one can interfere with our conversation.
Nothing.

Q: Will you answer more questions? Are you here?

We waited silently for a few minutes.
Al asked, "Do you notice communication is strong when we first start?"
"Now nothing," Jon added.
"It seems as if someone steps in and shuts us down," I stated.
We took a small break while Jon walked around the room. He finally regained communication, and we began again.

Q: What is the first letter of your first name?

A: The letter F was pointed out on its cue card.

Q: Are you afraid?

A: Yes.

Q: Did you live here?
A: Yes.

Q: Did you work here?
A: Powerful yes.

Q: Were you treated well?
A: No.

Q: Were you treated well by the owners?
A: No.

Q: Did many bad things occur in this house?
A: No.

Q: Did many bad things go on next door?
A: Yes, scared.

Q: Were abortions done on this property?
   No response.

Q: Did any of these things have to do with the boiler room?
A: Yes.

Q: Were you witness to these things?
A: Yes.

Q: Is it the guilt of these things that keeps you here?
A: No.

All of a sudden the back door slammed, and there was a banging noise coming from the first floor. Al went directly to the rear bedroom and peered out, but no one was there. He remained on watch as I went downstairs. I proceeded with caution, as I couldn't be sure of what I might find. I was more concerned about running into a living, breathing, intruder than one who was deceased. I checked the living room, and found nothing there. I moved on to the kitchen, checking the pantry and a nook by the back door. Nothing. I returned upstairs where I reported my findings to the others[6].

We went back to the front bedroom and continued.

Q: Is it the guilt that keeps you here?
A: No.

Q: Is it someone or something that keeps you earth-bound?
A: Yes.

Q: Someone?
A: Yes.

Q: Do you know Edward?
   No response.
A: Never mind!

Q: Are there things we need to know about the boiler room?
A: Yes.

Q: Did the present owners find anything when the old boilers were removed?
A: No.
   Scared, pause.

Q: Was the boiler room used to hide evidence of a crim...
A: Strong yes.

Q: Is there still evidence hiding there?
A: Yes.

Q: If we go to the boiler room, will you help us find this evidence?

A: Yes.

Q: You will direct us?
A: Yes.

Q: Is it buried?
A: No.

We were interrupted by a movement in the hall. Jon spotted it first, then I jumped up and fired a picture from my camera. Then nothing.

Q: Is it in the walls?
A: Yes.

Q: Near the chimney?
A: No.

Q: Near the coal bins?
A: Yes.

Q: In the coal bins?
A: No.

Q: Again, if we go to the boiler room, you will help us find this evidence?
A: Yes.

We set up our surveillance tapes throughout the upper portion of the house and departed.

We decided to take a break, and when we returned thirty-five minutes later, the house was quiet. We retrieved our equipment and headed down to the boiler room.

We spent an hour in the boiler room trying to communicate with the spirit, but there was too much interference from other spirits. The area was searched, but nothing was immediately found. There were a few places that we would have liked to inspect in more detail, but it would be impossible to do so without causing major damage to the building. We retired for the night and reviewed our tapes. It was interesting to note that the slamming of the back door, which so effectively interrupted our question and answer period, was not recorded on the tape; however, the same machine, recording in the same location, set at the same volume, recorded the door slamming shut as we left for our break.

chapter 20

W e entered the house, and, as usual, we waited and listened for a few minutes before proceeding. The house seemed quiet that night. Jon, Al, and I decided to assemble in the main floor living room. We had brought a chair with us for Jon, and he sat in the corner near the front wall of the house. I took out my gauss meter, and got an initial reading of zero milligauss, which is normal when there is no spirit activity. The temperature in the room was noted at 74.1° Fahrenheit. Al and I sat on the floor, on opposite sides of the room, and set up our tape recorders as Jon prepared himself. He began,

Q: We are here and wish to contact any spirit that is present. We are all here as friends. Is there a spirit here who wishes to speak with us?
A: Strong Yes.
"The power is strong tonight," Jon told us.

Q: Did you know of a woman who resided in this house named Angela?

A: Yes.

Q: Does this woman who was known as Angela have any living relatives within a fifty mile radius of this house?
A: Yes.

Q: Do these relatives still go by the same surname?
A: Yes.

Q: Would these relatives know of her?
A: Yes.

Q: Can you give us the first name of that relative?
A: Yes.

I laid out the cue cards with the letters of the alphabet, as well as the numbers from zero to ten, in three rows on the floor in front of Jon.

Q: Will you spell it out for us?
A: Yes.
The pendulum started off slowly, but as if there were some urgency, it sped up to the point of defying physics, and it would no longer wait for Jon. It not only pulled his hand along, but it also pointed at the next letter that it wanted us to record. Twice it went from a still position, pointing to a letter at a ten to twelve degree angle, to a reverse angle pointing at ten to twelve degrees. Note: a series of clicks and bangs not heard at the time were recorded on both tape systems, which were operating in different areas of the room, simultaneously.
We received the name.

Q: Can you give us a street address for this person?[7]
A: Yes.
We received the address.

Q: To clarify, this would be in the city of Toronto, Ontario, Canada?
A: Yes.

Q: Would you give us your name?
A: No.

Q: Will you answer any more questions for us?
No response.

Q: Do you wish to communicate further?
No answer.

Q: Are you still there?
Nothing.

We stopped for a break and continued an hour later.

Q: We are all here as friends; is there a spirit here who wishes to communicate with us?
A: Strong yes.

Q: Do you wish to show yourself?
A: No.

Q: Do you wish to communicate in a more direct manner?
A: No.

Q: Do you mind that we are here?
A: No.

Q: Will you answer any of our questions this evening?
A: Yes.

Q: Are you a spirit that resides here in this house?
A: No.

Q: Do you visit here often?
A: Yes.

Q: Do you have a special attachment to this place?
A: Yes.

Q: Do you wish to let us know what that attachment is?
A: No.

Q: Were you physical, in physical form, flesh and blood, here at one time?
A: No.

Q: Have you ever been in a physical form?
A: No.

Q: Are you of the light?
A: A weak yes.

Q: Do you seek to do good?
A: Yes.

Q: Is there something we can do for you?
    Communication stopped.
    Room temperature 76.2° F.
    Reading of 2 milligauss.

Q: Are you there?
A: Yes.

Q: Do you wish to communicate further?
A: Yes.

Q: Are you the one we were just talking with?
A: No.
    Pause.

Q: Are you happy here?
A: No.

Q: Are you unhappy because of the family that lives here?
A: No.

Q: Is there something that you want from Al?
A: Yes.

Q: To look for something?
A: Yes.

Q: Is it buried?
A: Yes.

Q: In this house?
A: No.

Q: In his house?
A: Yes.

Q: In the closet?
A: Yes.

Q: The same closet where the candle was thrown, and the door was opened?
A: Yes.
   Room temperature 79.6° F.
   Reading of 7 milligauss.

Q: If we dig and find something, will it be the end of these disturbances?
A: No.

Q: Are you the spirit that threw the cross in the bedroom?
A: Yes.

"If I've been harsh with you, it's because of the things you have been doing. I apologize"

Q: Did you hear what Al said?
A: Sensitive yes.

"You are always frightening my family. We can all get along. There is no need for what you have been doing."

Q: Do you hear?
A: Yes.

Q: Are there a young girl and woman among us?
A: Yes.

Q: Are these people your wife and daughter?
A: Yes.

"You and your family are welcome in my home as long as you do not cause any harm to my family."

Q: Al has said it is okay to reside within his house, but understand that you are not welcome in my home or in Richard's home at any time. Are you in this room at the present time?
A: Yes.
Room temperature 81° F.
Reading of 12 milligauss.

Q: Do you wish us to stop investigating?
A: No.

Q: Do you wish to join us now with your friends, to discuss anything at this time? Sit amongst us and communicate with us tonight.
A: Strong yes.

Al complains of a chill on his right side. The room temperature is 79.1° F. An isolated sweep of the right side of his location noted a temperature of 76° F.

"I'll be forty-nine this year; how old are you," Al asked to entice the spirit into further conversation.

Q: Were you born in the seventeenth century?
A: No.

Q: Nineteenth century?
A: No.

Q: Eighteenth century?
A: Yes.

Q: Late part of the eighteenth century?
A: Yes.

Q: Did you know the original owner of the property, a Mr. Henshaw?[8]
Jon had mispronounced the name, so we got no response.

Q: Did you know Mr. Henshaw?
No response. We later heard a male voice on the tape pronouncing the name correctly.

Q: Did you know Mr. Henshaw?
The same voice repeated the correct pronunciation.
A: Yes.

Q: Were you here during the war?
A: Yes.

Q: Were you a soldier?
Male voice on tape, "Yes."
A: Yes.

Q: Were you killed on this property?
Male voice on tape, "Yes."
A: Yes.

Jon became tired, so we stopped for a break.

Room temperature 66.7° F.

Reading of 10 milligauss.

Note: As Jon asked the questions, his voice activated my sound level meter into the sixty to seventy decibel range. I noticed that after the question, the meter indicated activity in the silence in the minus six to minus ten decibel range. We did not hear this activity at the time, but these voices were captured on the surveillance tapes.

We recommenced.

Room temperature 70.3° F.

Reading of 7 milligauss.

Q: So you were a soldier?

A: Yes.

Q: British?

A: No.

Q: American?

A: No.

Q: Canadian?

No response.

Q: Native?

A: Yes.

Q: You were in life Native of Canada?

A: Yes.

Q: Do you have some attachment to this property?

A: Yes.

Q: Are your remains buried here?

A: Yes.

Q: Are there others buried here?
A: Yes.

Q: Were these grounds sacred?
A: Yes.

Q: Were these grounds defiled?
A: Yes.

Q: Is this the reason for all these disruptions?
    A male voice, saying "Yes, leave me!" was later heard on the tape
A: Yes.

Q: Can we do something to help you?
    Same voice, "Yes."
A: Yes.

Q: Will you spell out what you want us to know, or to do?
A: Strong yes.
    E.A.R.T.H. was spelled out on the cue cards.

There were various clicks in the background recorded on the tapes, as well as a male voice saying "Ernie Heal!" We are still unsure whether this is Ernie's full name, or if he needs or wants to heal something — the earth, perhaps.

Q: What about the Earth?
A: S.A.C.R.E.D.

Q: Sacred Earth?
    Male voice, "Yes."
A: Yes.

I remembered seeing a plaque in the park[9] telling about Indian burial grounds in the area. I mentioned this to Al, who said, "They don't tell where, they just say in the area somewhere."

The pendulum started to swing, indicating "Yes." It gained speed, spinning like the blades of a helicopter. I began to fear for our safety. If Jon lost his grip, the pendulum would take off like a bullet.

Jon had to physically stop its movement. In the background, a male's voice asked, "Why?"

Q: Are you haunting these houses?
In the background, a different male's voice said, "Come here!"
A: Big yes.

Q: What do you want us to do?
A: D.I.G.

Q: You want us to dig?
A: Yes.

Q: Where?
A: D.U.G.
We paused to ponder what this meant.

Q: You want us to dig up what was dug up before?
A: Yes.

Q: You want us to find your remains?
A: Yes.

Q: If we do this, will the disturbances stop?
No response.

"He can't answer that, because he is not the only one causing problems," Jon told us.

Q: If we do this, will you be at rest?
A: Yes.

"Where did this Native come from? I mean, in the beginning it was the girl and the guy. We have a great deal of tapes with those two on them. This guy used to laugh behind my back!" Al exclaimed.

A male voice in the background on the tape could be heard laughing. Jon then said, "It could be all this energy. These disruptions are very powerful; there are so many spirits here, he just came to the front. I don't think he's harmful."

Q: Do you wish to answer any more questions?
A: No.

Q: Are you still here with us?
A: Weak yes.

Q: Are you tired?
A: Yes.

Q: Thank you; rest; go in peace. Is there any other spirit present who wishes to communicate with us?
A: No.

"It's getting cold in here again," Al remarked.

"The temperature's dropping. It's at 68°," I noted.

At this point, the tapes picked up an unknown male voice saying, "Help!"

chapter 21

Jon began his questioning again, and did something totally unexpected. He seemed somewhat angry.

Q: I understand yes and no. I want only truthful answers! Is there a spirit present who wishes to speak to us?
A: Yes.

Q: Do you need our assistance?
A: Yes.

Q: Are you the same spirit that we were talking with forty-five minutes ago?
A: No.

We heard several noises at the far end of our room, and also in the adjacent room.

Q: How many spirits are we dealing with, five?
A: Yes.

Q: Ten?
A: Yes.

Q: A hundred?
A: No.

Q: More than ten?
A: No.
   Room temperature 66.3° F.
   Reading of 12 milligauss.

Q: Do you want us to leave? Are we not welcome here?
A: No.

Q: Are you happy here?
A: No.

Q: Do you feel sad because you are not happy here?
Q: Are you going to cry?
Q: Are you trapped? Helpless? Angry? Frustrated?
A: Yes.

Q: You don't have to be here; you can move on to a better place. You
   don't have to be here. Move on. Do you feel you have unfinished
   business here?
   A male voice on the tapes says, "Yes."
A: Yes.

"It's just an excuse; they should leave. Seek out loved ones and go!
Do you stay because you are afraid to move on? Vacate! Leave! Go on to
somewhere else! We think you should get out! Quit hiding in this house;
don't be afraid to move on!"

The room felt electrified. Al broke into hysterics, laughing uncontrollably.

Whether it was nervousness, the stress of the moment, or something else, he could not explain. He tried to get up off the floor, but fell back down against the wall with his feet in the air — the laces on his boots had been tied together.

"I can't help it; every time he asks a question, something is making me laugh. I can't help it," Al tried to explain.

Jon continued, "All right, okay, you don't have to leave."

The pendulum went wild, spinning like the blades of a helicopter again. Jon had a difficult time holding it. There was concern that it would leave his hand and injure one of us.

"Thank you," Jon said as he stopped it with his other hand. "We are not here to kick you out, we are here to help. But we are getting frustrated too! This is your opportunity. It may be another two or three hundred years before anyone is even remotely interested in communicating with you. Give us a break; if you want us to help you, then you help us!"

Q: The lines of communication are open right now. Do you want us to help you?
A: Strong yes.

Q: Were you a Native Canadian?
A: Yes.

Q: Are your physical remains buried under this house?
   A male voice was recorded, saying "Yes."
A: Yes.

Q: Are they buried close to the surface of the earth?
A: Yes.

Q: Since your death, have you witnessed other murders on this property through the years?
   Male voice, "Yes."
A: Yes.

Q: Are some of those remains buried on this property as well?

Male voice, "Yes."

A: Yes.

Q: Are they present here in spirit as well?
Male voice, "Yes."

A: Yes.
Jon became tired at this point and ended the communication.

I met Al at his house. We wanted to get together to finish up with the house next door, but Jon was unable to make it. We decided to go next door for a while, before we went into the main underground tunnel.

We entered the house. It was dark and quiet. We stood in the kitchen for a few minutes listening, but there was nothing.

Al moved to the doorway of the living room. There came a low, but powerful, guttural growl from what seemed to be everywhere in the house. My gut instinct told me that it was time to leave, and that is what we did — we left immediately.

We entered the tunnel. Most of the lights were burnt out, so I turned on my flashlight. The light from its beam seemed to be absorbed by the blackness and only helped us see mere inches ahead of where we were walking. We spent some time looking around the room at the end of the tunnel, but we found nothing. We were about to leave when a gust of icy air came down the tunnel from nowhere, whipping past us. I took several photos, and we left the tunnel. The pictures turned out to be obscured by the blackness, despite the flash. They looked as if they had been taken under water. We also noticed that in two of the photos there were two dim red dots, like eyes peering out of the blackness. The remaining photos showed nothing like this.

The next day we inspected the tunnel, and found nothing that would have caused these red dots, just thick grey concrete walls. No wiring, pipes, or anything else that would have given off a reflection. The approximate height of these dots was 5'5" to 5'10" from the tunnel floor.

The news came from Al. The house next door had been rented, upon approval from the landlord. This meant that our time was limited as far as the investigation at this location was concerned. We all agreed to meet at the house as soon as possible.

It was late; the sun had already gone down when we met at the house. We assembled in the living room, on the main floor. I conducted a sweep of the main floor with the gauss meter, and found a reading of six milligauss near the door between the dining room and living room. It persisted for several seconds and then it was gone. I joined the others on the living room floor, handed Al a new tape, then set up my tape recorder. Jon began.

Q: You're among friends; is there any spirit present who wishes to communicate with us at this time? We wish you no harm, and this could be the last time we will be here. A woman will be moving in here soon; do you have a problem with this?
A: Yes.

Q: Feel free to speak; you're among friends. Did you see a young woman come into this house with the property manager the other day?
A: Yes.

Q: Will you rest while she lives here?
A: No.

Q: Will you attempt to influence her?
A: Yes.

Q: Is it within the realm of possibility that you will leave her in peace while she lives here?
A: No.

Q: The woman who moves in here will be making a lot of changes to this place — renovations — are you okay with this?
A: No.

Q: Are there more spirits than just you who have something to say about this?
A: Yes.

Q: Two?
A: Yes.

Q: Three?
A: Yes.

Q: Four?
A: Yes.

Q: Five?
A: Yes.

Q: Six?
A: Yes.

Q: Seven?
A: Yes.

Q: Eight?
A: Yes. The pendulum stopped.

Q: More than eight?
A: No.

Q: There are eight spirits here?
A: Yes.

Q: Are you all male energies?
No response to the question.

Q: Do you intend to do this woman harm?
A: Yes.

Q: Is there a particular reason you do not want people here?
A: Yes.

Q: Is it because you feel this property belongs to you?
A: Yes.

Q: Is there something here you do not want us to find?
A: Yes.

Q: This woman who is about to move in will do extensive renovations, is there something in this house you do not want her to find?
A: Yes.

Q: Will you interfere?
A: Yes.

Q: Will you defend what you feel is yours?
A: Yes.

Q: Do you know about this property, and the location of the underground tunnels?
A: No.

Q: Do you belong here, or are you just passing through? Just passing through?
A: Yes.
   Pause.

Q: With your permission, I would like to speak to just one spirit who has knowledge of this property. Will you allow this?
A: Yes.

Q: Thank you. Is there one spirit who has knowledge of this property who wishes to speak with us?
A: Yes.

Q: Is there a family gravesite of any owner throughout the history of this property located here?
A: Yes.

Q: Is this gravesite within the confines of the current property borders?
A: Yes.

Q: Is this gravesite closest to the lake or to the road? Closest to the lake?
A: Yes.

Q: Does this gravesite consist of more than one grave?
A: No.

Q: There is only one grave?
A: Yes.

Q: Was this grave marked?
A: Yes.

Q: Is the grave marked now?
A: No.

Q: Is it the fact that the grave is unmarked and unattended that makes you sad?
A: Yes.

Q: Is this grave yours?
A: Yes.

Q: Can you show us where your grave is?
A: Yes.

Jon introduced a map of the property and said, "Please show us on this map where your grave is located."

It was indicated that the grave lay on the stretch of grass between the small house by the lake and a low-rise building.

Q: Was you grave marker made of wood?
A: No.

Q: Stone?
A: Yes.

Q: Can you tell us what happened to the grave marker? Was it removed?
A: No.

Q: Was it covered over?
A: Yes.

Q: Was it deliberately sunk or buried?
A: Yes.

Q: Is it still close to the surface?
A: Yes.

Q: Was there ever a fence around your grave?
A: No.

Q: Did the owner of this property in 1905 know of the desecration of this grave?
A: Yes.

Q: Can you give us your first name?
A: Yes.
V.I.C.T.O.R.I.A. was spelled out on the cue cards.

Q: Can you give us your last name?
A: Yes.
B.E.S.T.

We stopped to discuss her name. A woman's voice on the tapes said "Come on," impatiently.

Q: Will you indicate the year you were born?
A: Yes.
1.7.9.8.

Q: Can you give us the year of your death?
A: Yes.
    1.8.4.3.

Q: Did you die of disease?
A: Yes.

Q: Tuberculosis? Consumption?
A: Yes.

Q: Did you live close by?
A: Yes.

Q: Are there those around you now that want to control this property?
A: Yes.

Q: Are they in conflict with each other?
A: Yes.
    The recordings revealed a woman's voice, crying "Help me!"

Q: Will you spell out any more for us?
A: Yes.
    I.L.E.A.V.E.

Jon said, "Thank you, Victoria Best; go in peace. We hope to speak again." The pendulum indicated "Yes," then nothing more. We concluded our sitting.

We tried on several occasions to investigate the gravesite pointed out by Victoria Best. However, there always seemed to be too many people around the area, and we didn't want to cause any problems for the property management.

Kellie and Shelby asked us to stop using electronic equipment in our investigation, as the devices clearly upset the spirits and this made the women fear for their safety. We agreed to stop all audio-visual surveillance, and though the activity didn't stop, they both felt better about the situation.

chapter 22

Kellie came downstairs one morning to get a drink and to read the morning paper. She found her dog lying in the doorway between the living room and the kitchen. The poor animal had died sometime during the night — likely as a result of something that the spirit did to it, though we're not positive of that. Through her tears she called Al down, and he wrapped the dog in a blanket and buried her in the yard. The next day Kellie heard the dog at the back door crying to be let out like she would normally do. This was extremely hurtful for Kellie, so we called Jon and asked him to come over, which he did. We all sat together and established contact.

Q: Do you know of the little dog that lived here that died recently?
A: Yes.

Q: Is the dog with you?
A: No.

Q: A dog was heard at the back door, was this the same dog?

A: No.

Q: We find this activity offensive and in extremely poor taste; it is hurtful to the family, and you will stop this activity now. Do you understand?"

A: Yes.

Jon thanked the spirit after their conversation, and the activity stopped. I felt that this event was probably just Edward using his ability to mimic so that he could play little hurtful tricks on the family.

The owner of the property stopped by and spoke with Jon about the basement of the mansion. He wanted to go over the information that we had gathered again. There seemed to be something bothering him, as if he were having second thoughts about his decision to stop our efforts and to redo the floor. The owner stated that the crew he had hired to fix the floor were all professional contractors who he had used for a number of years to build and fix up properties that he owned, but on this particular job, they had had a great deal of difficulty in completing their task. They had to repair the floor seven times before it was completed. Each time the job appeared to be finished, something would occur. The floor would be levelled and left to dry, only to be found the next day to be warped and bent at odd angles; or it was cracked, sometimes with water coming up though the holes; or it had sinking spots. Jon looked at him and asked, "Doesn't this tell you something?"

He agreed, but wouldn't commit to any further action. There was something more bothering him. He was starting to have unexplained problems at home, as well. We only hoped that he would eventually realize that it was our responsibility — and his — to resolve this situation.

The issue was later raised about the possibility that the owner was being externally influenced and made to change his mind in the first place. Of course, we couldn't prove or disprove this idea either way.

It was noted that as interesting as our contact with all of these spirits was, we couldn't help but feel that they were being pushed to the forefront to act as a diversion from the real mystery that we were trying to solve.

Where were the original players that had started all of this? Could it be that Edward had been telling the truth when he said that he was in complete control of this property? Was he using the other spirits to take up our time and confuse the real issues? We believed so. We all agreed that we had to get back on the right track.

I have found, through my experiments in EVP, that the volume on the recording equipment has to be set at close to maximum. Unfortunately, this produces background static, or white noise. I feel that this noise is the carrier wave for the spirits' communication, at least when that communication involves electronic equipment. I have attempted to reduce, and even to remove, this static by lowering the volume, by employing more sophisticated recording systems, and by adding noise filters. The results have always been extremely poor. For example, we ran a test in the servants' residence using a very expensive high-tech recording system, with one of our microcassette recorders placed a foot away from the device. We set both up to record with new tapes, and the house was vacated and secured. After enough time had elapsed for the tapes to run out, they were retrieved and reviewed. The high-tech system produced nothing, while the microcassette recorder captured movement, talking, and whispers.

chapter 23

J on began.

Q: Remember, you are among friends, and we wish you no harm. Is there a spirit here who wishes to communicate?
A: Immediate yes comes through.

Q: Is this the energy of a male or a female? Male?
A: Yes.

Q: You may speak freely; were you ever in a physical form, that of a living person?
A: Yes.

Q: Do you cling to this house or property on a regular basis?
A: Yes.

Q: Did you live on, or near to, this property?
A: No.

Q: Were you stationed here?
A: Yes.

Q: 1812?
A: Yes.

Q: Was there a battle or conflict here?
A: No.

Q: Do you know Victoria Best?
A: No.

Q: Were you part of the British Forces?
A: Yes.

Q: Were you born in Britain?
A: Yes.

Q: Did you die here?
A: Yes.

Q: Are your remains still here?
A: Yes.

Q: Are you familiar with Fort York?
A: Big yes.

Q: Can you give us your first name?
A: Yes.
   T.E.D.

Q: Your first name is Ted?
A: Yes.

Q: Can you give us your last name?
A: Yes.
  Filmore or Filmoore was said, though we couldn't make out which.

Q: Thank you. Can you give us your rank?
A: Yes.
  S.E.A.M.A.N.

Q: Can you give us the name of your unit?
A: Yes.
  H.E.R. M.A.J.E.S.T.Y.S. R.O.Y.A.L. N.A.V.Y.

Q: You served in the navy?
A: Yes.

Q: Can you give us the name of the ship you served on?
A: Yes.

  There was some confusion, as we were getting Prince William, while the surveillance tape was recording a male's voice stating "Prince Henry."

Q: Did you die on land?
A: Yes.

Q: Did you die in battle?
A: No.

Q: In an accident?
A: No.

Q: From illness?
A: Small yes.

Q: You are not happy with the way that you died. Would you have rather died in battle?
A: Yes.

Statement: We can't choose the way we are to go; you served your country well, please go in peace and rest. Thank you, Ted Filmore.

We entered the middle townhouse and again situated ourselves in the front room. This was the last meeting that we would hold here, as the house was about to be rented. Jon arranged the lawn chairs that we had brought with us as Al set up the folding table and I lit the candles. The house was deathly quiet as we took our positions. Al and I loaded new tapes into the recording equipment and waited for Jon to begin.

Q: Is there a spirit present who wishes to communicate with us tonight?
A: Yes.

Q: When you were physical were you that of a male, were you a man?
A: Yes.

Q: Can you give us your name?
A: Yes.

Q: Please spell it out for us, starting with your first name.
A: V.I.C.T.O.R.

Q: Your first name is Victor?
A: Yes.

Q: Can you please spell your surname for us?
A: Yes.
   M.O.O.R.E.

Q: Did you work on this property?
A: Yes.

Q: Were you one of the people who built this property?
A: Yes.

Q: Did you work for George?
A: No.

Q: Did you work for Harry?
A: Yes.

Q: Can you tell us why you are here?
A: Dead.

Q: You're here because you're dead?
A: Yes.

Q: Victor, were you a tradesman who helped build the mansion?
A: Yes.

Q: Did you die on this property?
A: Yes.

Q: Tell us how you died, Victor.
A: Heart.

Q: You had a heart attack?
A: Yes.

Q: Can you give us the year of your death?
A: Yes.
    1.9.0.7.

Q: Why are you here? We understand that you're dead, but why do you
    remain here?
A: Work.

Q: You have work to do here?
A: Yes.

Q: Victor can you tell us what year it is?

A: Yes
2.0.0.1.
Pause.

Q: Are there any other spirits here with you on this property?
A: Yes.

Q: How many others?
A: Seven.

Q: There are seven others besides you?
A: Yes.

Q: How many of those spirits are female?
A: One.

Q: Are any of these spirits friendly?
A: No.

Q: Out of all these spirits, none are nice?
A: None.

Q: Just you; you're the only nice one Victor?
A: Yes.

Q: Is there one spirit amongst this group who seems to be in control of the others?
A: Yes.

Q: Do they make it difficult for you?
A: Yes.

Q: Do they interfere with your work?
A: Yes.

Q: The energy who seems to be in control of the others, is he known by a name?

A: Yes.

Q: Can you give us his name?

A: Yes. Edward.

Q: Please give us his last name?

A: S.A.L.I.N.A.S.

Q: Do you know what Edward did here when he was living? What his job or employment was?

A: Janitor.

Q: Can you tell us anything about Edward?

A: Bad.

Q: Is he here with us now?

A: No.

Q: Do you know where he is right now?

A: Attic.

Q: In the main house?

A: Yes.

Q: Victor do you know the name of the woman here? Can you give us her name?

A: Angela
   Pause.

Q: Victor, are you still here?
   Nothing.

Q: Victor, are you still here?
   No response.

Q: Who has just arrived in this house? Please identify yourself.
A: F.U.

Q: Edward, is that you?
A: 1.

Q: Edward, will you speak with us on an intelligent level? We wish you
no harm, we only seek information. Can you tell us why you still walk
this property?
A: Nuts.

Q: Who's nuts?
No response.

Q: Do you feel you were abandoned here?
A: Coward.

Q: Who's a coward? You're afraid to move on?
A: U. R. Coward.

Q: We are here speaking with you. Can you see us sitting here, can you,
do you have that ability?
A: Ass.

Q: You're the one who hides in the shadows, behind corners!
A: F.U. F.U. F.U. . . .
"We're not getting anywhere here!" Jon exclaimed.

Q: Okay, seriously, is there anything you want to tell us? Are you afraid?
Lonely? Do you want us to leave you alone?
A: Eat shit!

Q: Do you remember when George went to jail and the government sent
a person down to take control of the property?
A male voice uttering the word "shit" was recorded at this point.
A: Prick.

Q: Yes he was; he got in your way, ruined your plans.
A: Prick.

Q: All of us in this room are of Italian background.
A: W.O.P.

Q: Do you ever see Mary?
A: Yes.

Q: Is she a wop too?
A: Yes.

Q: Are you the one who goes to Al's house?
A: Yes.

Q: Why do you go there?
A: Mine.

Q: Are there spirits there that you still go and see?
A: Nice.

Q: What do you mean, "nice"?
   No response.

   "We are going to speak with your boss now!"
   Edward's voice appeared on the tape, saying "Geo . . . George!"
   Pause.

Q: Do you remember the girl that lived in the house who you used to chase?
A: No.

Q: Come on, we were all there; the girl who gave us your name?
A: No.

Q: Why did you throw the crucifix across the room?

A: No.

Q: Are you religious? Do you have any faith?
A: F.U.

Q: Is there anything that you wish to tell us?
A: Bye.

"Bye, Edward."

chapter 24

Jon was trying to work in his office, a converted sunroom at the front of the main floor of the mansion, when he was distracted by a loud thumping above his head. It was coming from the apartment directly above his. He watched the pictures on his walls vibrate with each thump and became annoyed, but since it was during the day, he just shrugged it off and tried to focus on his work. The next morning, he was awoken by the same noises and decided that he would speak to management to see if something could be done. Again that evening, the thumping started up. He had not spoken to the management yet, and decided to go upstairs himself to see what his neighbour was doing.

As he stepped out of his apartment, he was surprised to see his neighbour coming in the front door from the parking lot. He stopped her and told her what he had heard. She told him that she lived there alone, and that no one should be in her unit. She also told him that she would give him a key and asked that he investigate if he ever heard anything in her apartment during the day.

Victor had said that he hadn't finished his work, which was to build the mansion. Was it possible that what Jon was hearing was Victor building? We discussed this at one of our meetings, and remembered one of our surveillance tapes that had recorded the sounds of lumber being tossed onto the floor and sounds of contractors building something.

Shelby took the information provided by Victor and found his name in the Government archives. We thought that this seemingly minor incident might prove to be significant all on its own. We had contacted an energy that no one in our group ever knew existed, yet the information that he gave us was verifiable and real. We decided at that point to conduct a test to ensure that what we were receiving was not some type of influence from within our group, but actual external information. After a short discussion, we came up with a plan. Al would have to find a vacant apartment for us to be able to implement it, though.

When an apartment became available, we received three pieces of information about it: firstly, it was vacant; secondly, one of the occupants had died, and his wife had gone off to live with family; and lastly, we knew the surname of the recent residents. Jon wouldn't be given any of this information.

We assembled at Al's to prepare for our test. The three of us then went to the vacant apartment and set up in the living room. Jon began, and we made contact quickly. Within minutes we had received the first names of both the spirit and his wife, the year that they had moved in and the length of time that they had lived there, and where his wife had moved to, as well as a great deal of peripheral information. We left the apartment that night not knowing if anything at all had been accomplished, and for a week I wondered about this simple test until Susan provided the data that we were looking for. Each piece of information that was collected was correct. We now knew that we were collecting viable, confirmable information.

We sat in the living room, which was empty except for the two candles that provided us with a little bit of light. Jon was trying to focus. He was breathing heavily. He looked up at Al and I and said, "There may be trouble here tonight." I felt it as well, but I kept the feeling to myself. Jon began:

Q: Is there a spirit here who wishes to communicate?

A: Yes.

Q: Are you attached to this place?
A: No.

Q: Were you ever in the physical?
A: No.

Q: Are you just passing through?
A: Yes.

Communication stopped. All was quiet, as the three of us scanned the room. Although there was no change in the brightness of the candle flames, the room grew darker, as if something had descended upon us.

Q: Is there a spirit here?
A: Very powerful Yes.

Q: Are you the one that we were just talking with?
A: No.

Q: Are you a friend?
A: Extremely weak Yes.

Q: Have we been in contact with you before?
A: Yes.

Q: Edward?
A: Yes.

Q: Do you wish to communicate with Richard?
A: Powerful Yes.

Q: Are you upset with Richard?
A: Yes.

Q: Is there something Richard has done to upset you?
A: Yes.

Q: Is it because he keeps digging around?
A: Yes.

Q: Do you wish he would go away?
A: Yes.
The power in the responses was growing to a fevered pitch; I felt that the pendulum might fly out of Jon's hand and injure one of us.

Q: Do you want us to get rid of him for you?
A: Yes, yes, yes.

Q: Well, tough. He is going to be around for a long time, digging into your affairs. What do you think about that?
Jon had to stop the pendulum. After a few moments, he continued:

Q: Did you know George when he was alive?
A: Yes.

Q: Did you have anything to do with Alvin[10]?
A: Yes.

Q: Did you supply the booze to him?
A: Yes.

Q: Was he the one who sent his men to the estate to extort money from your boss?
A: Yes.

Q: You're upset with George?
A: Yes.

Q: You never got what was promised to you? You got ripped off?
A: Yes.

Q: Did you go to Alvin's house and extract your pound of flesh?
A: Yes.

Q: Was it George's idea to hit Alvin for what he did?
A: Yes.

Q: The girl in the basement, did you kill her?

The pendulum stopped dead from a powerful clockwise movement, then started moving in the opposite direction, tracing out a pentagram.

Jon just stared at it as if someone else were holding it, "I've never seen it do this before!"

"Stop it, stop . . ." I yelled at Jon.

Jon grabbed it with his other hand and stopped it. Several unidentifiable noises appeared on the tapes while all of this was occurring. We waited a few moments for Jon to calm himself, and then he continued:

Q: We are here as friends, we wish you no harm, and we are not here to make you leave. It's truth-telling time — did you kill her?
A: Yes.

"Can you give an audible sign, like you used to do at my house?" Al asked.
A: My house!

Q: Did you go back to Alvin's house to kill someone?
A: No.

Q: Do you know the spirit at Alvin's old house?
A: Yes.

Q: Is he a friend?
A: No.

Q: Did he die of natural causes?
A: No.

Q: Was he connected to Alvin?

A: Yes.

Q: Was he your contact man?
A: No.

Q: Is it Alvin?
A: No.

Q: Did you run booze to Buffalo?
A: Yes.

Q: Good cash?
A: Yes.

Q: Were people tossed overboard into the lake?
A: Yes.

Q: To their deaths?
A: Yes.

Q: Where is your flock, next door watching the birthday party?
A: Yes.

Q: Did Alvin want you to work for him?
A: Yes.

Q: Did you?
A: No.
    We stopped our question period there.

We entered the main house and climbed the stairs to the second floor. We paused at the door that was at the end of the long hallway. We entered his room. It was small and cramped, as the roof angled in to a peak. On both sides were tiny hatches for access into the lower attic. We quickly found a place to sit and prepared to begin.

Q: We are here as friends; is there a spirit here who wishes to communicate?
A: Yes.

Q: Is this Edward?
A: No.

Q: Have we ever spoken before?
A: No.

Q: Were you a male in life?
A: No.

Q: Were you a female in life?
A: No.

Q: Were you ever physical?
A: No.

Q: Who are you? Will you give us your name?
A: Yes. Bucca.

Q: Why are you here? Did you come here on your own?
A: No.

Q: Were you brought here?
A: Yes.

Q: By George?
A: No.

Q: By Harry?
A: Yes.

Q: Why don't you go home?
A: No home.

Q: Why do you stay here?
   No reply.

Q: Do you have to?
A: No.

Q: Do you like it?
A: Yes.

Q: Are you in control of what goes on here?
A: Yes.

Q: Are you in control of Edward?
A: Yes.

Q: Do you wish us harm?
A: No

Q: Is the courtyard a monument to you?[11]
A: Yes.

Q: Built by Harry?
A: Yes.

Q: Did he perform rituals here?
A: Yes.

Q: Did people die as a result of these rituals?
A: No.

Q: Is this how he brought you here?
A: Yes.

Q: Are you in control of all of the others here?
A: Yes.
   Thank you.

chapter 25

So the mystery seemed to be solved, at least for this particular house. Edward had lived and worked as a loyal subject to his friend and boss. He had a hidden closeness to this man, whom he idolized and looked up to as a father figure. He would do almost anything for him, and because of this relationship he did questionable things and committed criminal acts. He wanted to follow in his boss's footsteps.

He was introduced to this gangster, Alvin, and became the middle-man, responsible for arranging deliveries and collecting money. Alvin liked this young man and respected the loyalty that he showed to his boss. He was the type of man that Alvin could use in his own organization. Alvin approached Edward with a business proposition and Edward turned him down, remaining loyal to his boss. Alvin's ego was damaged. How could anyone turn down such a generous offer? Alvin finally saw an opportunity to compromise Edward's integrity in his boss's eyes, and set him up. His boss was angered, and although he kept Edward on his staff, he was no longer trusted.

Edward remained loyal though, and after his death he came back to the only home that he ever felt comfortable living in, and met the others. He took control over the property, in hopes of once again proving his loyalty to his boss.

But this is where it gets complicated. It seems that the personalities of Edward and the one known as Bucca have merged to form a very powerful force that maintains a tight control and influence over the property and those who live on it. One is fuelled by the other's anger and hurt, and together they are a dangerous combination for the residents.

With the addition of a new baby into the family, it became evident that it would be impossible to remain in this house. The baby couldn't be left out of eyesight for a moment. Even when Al and Kellie slept next to the crib, toys and household items would manage to find their way into it with the baby, or the infant would be somehow startled out of a sound sleep. Al and Kellie decided to leave the house. Once they had made their choice to get out and actively began searching for a new residence, the activity in their house increased.

There was a final great push to ensure that they didn't change their minds. The forces in the house began to show themselves more often: a small white figure, that of a child, ran from the main floor bathroom to the stairs, then disappeared; items were openly being thrown at Kellie and her cousin Rebecca, who had come over for a visit.

They obtained an apartment through the management office and quickly packed, taking loads over to the new place every day.

It was early morning when the dark figure made his final appearance to Kellie. As she knelt beside the bathroom tub, bathing the baby, something moved in her peripheral vision. She looked up as the apparition glided past the open bathroom door a mere two feet from where she knelt. It disappeared toward the stairs. Kellie grabbed the baby and retreated to the bedroom, placing an emergency call to Al. He came home immediately and found nothing out of the ordinary. The move took place without further incident.

The spirits had won. The house was now empty, but that would be short lived. New tenants would be coming. A work team went in to prepare the house with plaster and fresh paint, but their inspection lasted only a few minutes as they heard someone walking above their heads. They ended up out front, standing in the roadway. It appeared that the landlord would have to bring in an outside firm to prepare this one.

From time to time one of us will pass by and look up at the windows; they sit empty and dark, gazing back indifferently.

epilogue

Science is, in essence, a meticulous study of phenomena. This study leads to the development of new thoughts and formulas, new types of equipment, and, ultimately, to an explanation for phenomena, with data to support each theory or solution. Throughout history, many examples can be found of observations and ideas that were once thought to be ridiculous — even mad — only to be proven true. These observations have allowed us to progress as a species and to learn about our world. A lot of ideas and theories from the past were at one time considered ludicrous — from the world being round, to our ancestors trying to throw rocks at the moon, to putting a man on it. Imagine if we had burnt Edison at the stake for creating the phonograph with its talking disk!

Yet modern scientists have a seemingly unchangeable outlook when it comes to claims of life after death. This may be due to the research that is being done, and the information that we present as fact or evidence. This idea seems to have been overlooked for the vast majority of paranormal investigations in the past, as it pertains to ghosts. It appears that most researchers have sought out the events, half-heartedly made notes, possibly taken some photos, and then moved on to the next event; never spending the time or energy needed to find the hard answers; producing nothing more than a collection of short stories. Granted, these stories are interesting to read and provide important background material, but they rarely bring us closer to an understanding of what is actually taking place.

Because very little progress has been made in the field of the paranormal over so many years, those before us have found a need to over-complicate the study of ghosts. This allowed them a justification for the frustrations that they were faced with in their investigations. Those who twisted their findings to fit their personal belief systems had little chance of truly discovering something new. An investigation doesn't stand a chance if the investigator goes into the field with a closed mind. How can one have a clear picture and a conclusion as to what is occurring prior to knowing about the event itself?

The easy road has been taken for far too long. Too many times I have seen an investigator cramming an event into an old theory, even though it didn't fit. We can't even agree on what to call them — ghosts, spirits, souls, spectres, spooks, phantoms, or poltergeists — which lends its hand to creating further confusion. Whatever you call them, they are simply people who have been removed from their bodies through death, and who exist in a state of intelligent energy, hovering just beyond our perception.

These same investigators attempt to assign specific attributes and characteristics to each being, stating that if it *does* one sort of thing, then it can only *be* one sort of thing. For example, if it throws things at you, then it must be a poltergeist; but if you see it, it would be something totally different, like an apparition; but then it depends on what it's doing, and how it acts and/or reacts. The point is that they are simply dead. Their actions, reactions, and activities are as random and as plentiful as those of the living. They have a great deal of time on their hands, as time means relatively nothing to them, and they can demonstrate wants, needs, and emotions, especially if the attachment to their past life remains strong.

The descriptive variation between ghost and poltergeist is vast; however, from what was demonstrated in this haunting, the two are one and the same. It seems that in the past the need to categorize each haunting with a specific name was so great that from the moment it happened the investigation was doomed.

I wrote to a well-known ghost hunter in the US, and explained that I was working on a procedure for pulling ghosts out into the open to record them and their actions. I further explained that during this procedure the positive results could be replaced with a short-lived poltergeist outburst. This was due to the method of manipulating the individual's memory. Simply put, if the memory response was a good one, the results were a photograph, a tape recording, or some other type of recordable activity. If the memory response was painful, or brought on feelings of anger or frustration, then you could expect poltergeist activity, resulting in damage and/or injury. He refused to contact me, as it was beyond his comprehension and training to admit that at one moment it was a ghost and at the next it was a poltergeist. It's this thinking that tries to neatly separate and package each episode with its own title that makes advancements difficult. They are adamant that a ghost cannot be a poltergeist. People are people, dead or alive, and that includes all of the attributes related to feelings and emotions. Ghosts are what they are, and poltergeist activity is simply a by-product of their anger and frustration.

It is like having two children; regardless of how they act, they are still your children, and you would introduce them as such. Some researchers, however, would apparently introduce their children as "this is my child the ghost, and this is my brat the poltergeist."

One of the other topics that I discussed with a local scientist was that poltergeists focus on adolescents coming into puberty. They somehow manifest poltergeist activities with their minds fired up by raging hormones. Thus, some believe that puberty causes poltergeist activity. This is a long-standing and widely accepted theory. However, what we found in this investigation was that even though there was a young child involved, the activity continued when she was removed from the environment.

Other investigations have suggested that activity only occurs when there is conflict within the family unit, so our environment was controlled to ensure that there was no conflict. But even if there had been conflict and it was hidden, or of a subconscious nature, it wouldn't explain why the activity occurred when the dwelling was devoid of all living people.

A third suggestion is that poltergeist activity centres on a person, not a place. However, even if someone in this family unit had produced the poltergeist activity, it still would not explain the several accounts from previous tenants, dating back to the year 1950, who reported the same type of activity.

Poltergeist simply means noisy ghost, and a ghost is just a ghost, just as people are people, alive or dead. There are as many personalities as there are individuals. Poltergeist activity is expressed by a spirit out of frustration or anger (see chart in Annex I). If a person didn't express these emotions strongly in life, they likely wouldn't do so in death, either.

It seems that our knowledge of the world's technology ends at the time of our deaths. For example, an individual who died prior to the invention of the microcassette recorder would not know how to operate one. This held true when the male spirit discovered the recorder operating in the master bedroom. He picked it up from the top of the dresser where we had set it. The device recorded his fumbling over the microphone before he threw it onto the bed and swore at it out of pure frustration. However, the first tape recording made in the house involving the young girl was quite different. Once she detected it, she was able to turn off the device without any trouble at all. This is at least one of the reasons for the male spirit to pursue her. He knew that she could provide a great deal of information to him about the modern world.

It was noted on several occasions that the male spirit demonstrated an inability to learn how to operate our equipment. This led me to believe that spirits do not see things in the physical world the same way that we do. He didn't possess the ability to learn simple operating techniques, even through he observed us using the equipment on a daily basis. It wasn't until after that Saturday night, after the pursuit and apparent capture of the girl, that he began interfering with our equipment. If he did indeed use her to teach him about modern electronics, then this would also indicate the existence of social interaction among spirits, be it positive or negative.

The interaction between male and female spirits was ever-present, though it was extremely difficult for us to make contact with the female spirits. It seemed as if they were stifled, or even controlled, by the males. They did speak among themselves — their whispers were picked up in the background — but as they came forward, it was almost exclusively the males who would speak with us.

Another interesting observation that was made on several occasions was what I call "insertion," which is similar to telepathy. I believe that insertion was the reason that most relationships in the mansion failed. Insertion happens when a spirit projects a sound or a voice directly into the mind of a specific person, or a specific group of people. It can also occur that a group of people in the same location, at the same time, will each report that the content of the message that they heard is different from what the others heard. However, the content of these messages can cause each person to react as if a different person had initiated the action requiring a response. For example, Kellie was upstairs and Shelby was downstairs; each heard the other call them, and each responded to the other, asking what was wanted. Neither, of course, had actually called the other.

Another example of this was the night that Jon, Al, and I were conducting our investigation in the vacant house next door to Al's. We were in the middle of an intense line of questioning when our attention was diverted by the sound of the back door of the house slamming. Our immediate response was to look into the incident, but we found that there was no one there. Our surveillance tapes clearly depict us moving in response to the sound. All three of us heard the sound, yet it was not captured on our tapes. When we left for a break, though, we left the tapes running in the same locations that they had been in when that incident occurred, and they recorded both our departure and the sound of the door closing.

Spirits seem to know when equipment is operating within their vicinity. They can zero in on its location, even if it is hidden. They also have the ability to avoid detection if they wish, or to tamper with the device or interact with it, as was the case with the camcorder operating in the master bedroom. The camera was hidden under a pile of clothing; the microphone and lens were slightly exposed, pointing down the hall toward the bathroom. The spirit would position itself just off-camera and tap on the microphone or push the side of the camera. Spirits can also remain hidden from the unblinking eye of the camera lens. On one of our videotapes, the audio portion records someone walking down the hall and knocking at the bathroom door, which we had left closed. The video portion of the tape shows only stringy shadows moving down the hall, pressed against the wall. Then the doorknob turns and the bathroom door opens. A bright light is seen from the hinged side of the door, coming from inside the room through the gap, and then the door swings slightly closed.

If this game of hide-and-seek isn't frustrating enough for investigators, the spirits will play with them to create an even greater sense of mystery and confusion. They have the absolutely clear intention of not co-operating with an investigation. They will lead people in various directions, but whether it is the right direction is anybody's guess. Early on in our investigation, we were discussing a possible theory when a male's voice, directly behind us, whispered, "That's not it!" It was very smug.

Something to be careful of, which we found out the hard way, is people professing to be mediums. We were extremely lucky to be put into contact with the first medium, who assisted the young girl in her escape from the house. However, because of her health, she would not return to deal with the others. A new team, recommended by a mutual friend, came to the house. They said that they would help us solve the situation, and that they would rid the house of spirits. They put on an interesting show; however, they were obvious frauds. They needed far too much background information, which we provided — though some was real and some false. The "mediums" played mostly on the false information, because it seemed more interesting to them. If we had not been suspicious of them, we might have followed the information that they were feeding us, thus leading us away from the discovery of valuable information, and further distorting the truth of what was actually occurring.

Should one ever have to deal with these people, their backgrounds should be investigated thoroughly and their records checked for accuracy. In the case of the first medium that we dealt with, she felt that it was important to assist us for the safety of the young girl. She refused all money that was offered to her and to her church. Even when Kellie mailed a cheque to the church it was returned to her. The second medium that came to the house was more interested in the money than anything else; she was paid one hundred dollars for her services.

I believe that prior to death there is a time of preparation by the other side to receive the dying. For example, there are thousands of documented cases of terminally ill people who, on their deathbeds, seem to acknowledge people unseen by others present by pointing at, nodding responses to, and answering unheard questions from them. This "briefing," as I call it, comforts and prepares the dying individual for the traumatic change which is about to come, and assists in their transition from life to afterlife. Even in ancient religious beliefs there are references to what is called a psychopomp — a guide who meets the dying to comfort and prepare them for the journey into the spirit world. The psychopomp is normally a deceased parent or other close relative who will be recognizable to the dying, and who will know all about them. This person will guide them to where they need to be.

With a suicide, as in the case of this young girl, the passing is unexpected and therefore no one is prepared to meet her. It wasn't her time to die, and her guide wasn't there, so the girl became lost. Then she did what came naturally: she went home to the place that she knew and loved, expecting to find that nothing had changed. Her loneliness and fear became tools of deceit for the male spirit in the house when he caught her. He explained to her that suicide was a sin, and that she had to choose either to stay with him, or to go to hell. The girl, having been raised in the Catholic belief system, found it easy to believe what he was telling her.

Why are they here, all around us? It seems that there isn't anywhere for them to go, as they exist in their own reality, which overshadows ours. Heaven and hell are not specific places, but rather a frame of mind. They are what we create for ourselves. For those who pass over in peace, they move on to join dearly departed relatives that have gone on before them. For those not at peace, they create their own hell, one fuelled by fear, guilt, greed, and the evil deeds committed in life. They become their own tormentors, clinging to the edges of reality in the present time; dwelling, hiding, hoping that they will not be seen for what they really are. Religions have painted horrible pictures of hell, so these spirits feel that if they move on, a far worse place awaits them. People who are at peace are dead to them. As the living wait for a birth to carry on the life cycle, they wait for death to bring their loved ones to them.

Since they exist in extremely close proximity to our own reality, separated only by a thin membrane, we receive intuition, déjà vu, images, and other information from the other side, and they can pass through this membrane into our reality. These realities are based on a time frequency, theirs being slightly different from our own. Science has shown us that everything has a specific frequency. Human life operates on several different frequencies, but in death, these frequencies are slightly elevated, vibrating at a level that we cannot see or hear. When spirits are laden with strong emotions (fear, guilt, helplessness, or wanting, for example), these negative feelings send them into a depression, reducing their frequencies. Thus, their actions start to appear in our reality in the form of sights and sounds. It seems that our bodies act as an insulator, like the rubber around an electrical wire. As we die, and the body is shed, the spirit being released is elevated in frequency. Psychic ability is simply an example of an individual who can tune-in to this higher frequency.

There has been a lot of good work in the field of electronic voice phenomena, where investigators — including Edison, von Szalay, Juergenson, Raudive, and Marconi — have tapped into this frequency with relative success. The spirits are there, and they will communicate with us, but we have to reach beyond this barrier. Edison, Bell, and Marconi all believed that we could, and experimented in developing methods to communicate with the deceased.

project psycho-trap

Paranormal investigation is not readily accepted by the scientific community and, in fact, is normally dismissed and ridiculed by the academic world at large. This is largely due to many of the theories that have been developed over the years — theories that have stood solidly, without question, and are unfortunately followed by researchers, leading them down the wrong path. Had these theories been questioned, new hypotheses relating to their investigations could have been made, and new discoveries may have been brought forth. I have heard and read many references in which investigators describe supernatural events that imprint themselves into the environment, only to be released at a later date to play over and over like a video loop. I have been a witness to these events, and they do appear to be images from the past.

However, I now have to disagree with this theory. We are all creatures of habit, and even though a spirit can come and go as it pleases, it will still punctuate an upset or angered feeling toward the living by slamming a door upon exiting. This could simply be a show of frustration at the communication barrier. It was this type of activity that made me think that even though spirits have passed over, they may still hold onto habits and belief systems learned in life. If this is true, then quite possibly they are social beings, and if so, it shouldn't pose too great a problem to modify existing psychological experiments to see how they will react.

From what was learned in an investigation that I have been working on for the past several years, a great deal of these events (sights/sounds) are past events, but they are not imprinted into the environment at all. They are the memories of actual spirits who, at times of deep thought, remember times in their lives that invoke such powerful emotions of joy or sadness that the memory manifests itself as sight, sound, or both, and is projected into our reality, thus creating a phantom or a ghost. The projection of those sounds and images comes directly from the spirit's mind. The images are not a true haunting, as they are simply carrying out a past event from the life of the deceased. They have nothing to do with us, or our present time period. These events or memories will simply act out, just as they happened in the past. They are without any real substance and cannot interact with us. What we are seeing is a piece of history from that individual's past. We must remember that the spirit isn't very far away from these events. From the information collected, it seems that spirits spend a great deal of time in thought, or what I call living memory, as these phantoms are quite common.

In another haunting that I investigated, on several occasions there seemed to be a loud party in progress. There were many voices, the clinking of glasses, laughing, and carrying on. One might think that there were many spirits there at this particular event, but it was only one. Its memory of the party invoked such a powerful feeling that it manifested itself into sound in our reality. Had this spirit been that of a close relative, it wouldn't be surprising to hear yourself amongst the ghostly party, as you could have been part of that memory.

What we collected in the investigation detailed in this book are the young girl's memories: discussions, arguments with her mother, the calling of her dogs' names, the sounds of their barking, and knowledge of the disturbing and horrific events that she went through in her short life. We know that these recordings are her memories, as we hear both sides of the conversation.

The voices in these recordings have been confirmed both by other tapes that we had of her voice and by people who knew her well. We also know that her mother, her dogs, and other people on the tapes are still alive. We know, too, that her spirit was in the house, as it interacted with people and objects. There are also a great deal of sounds of things breaking and being moved or damaged when, in fact, there is no evidence to suggest that anything like this physically occurred while we were there. This again is part of the memory process.

An image that plays over and over has a strong emotional significance to the spirit, or formulates a problem or mystery to that spirit. Just as we go over problems in our own heads, sometimes many times before we come to a conclusion, a spirit will also play out the last days or hours of its life, trying to solve the biggest mystery of all, as it may not have come to terms with its own death. Or, in the event of an unexpected death or suicide, it may not even realize that it is dead. The spirit would then have to work out the incidents leading to its death, and ultimately the event that followed.

Through my studies I have learned that it is possible to trigger ghostly events that can be studied. These events will mean nothing, however, if paranormal investigators rush the procedure and fail to do their homework. Also, the scientific community has to meet us halfway. We can't bring these projects into the lab to study under a microscope — it's all fieldwork. However, once a location is established to conduct a test, the area can be stringently controlled.

An investigator must conduct a great deal of study on each individual case. Determining the identity of the spirit, where possible, is of utmost importance. If this can be achieved, then a full background check of this individual should be undertaken. Once this information is collected, the investigator can attempt to replicate an environment and event of extreme happiness or sadness that will relate specifically to the spirit being investigated. Having done this, it should trigger a memory response that will manifest itself in our reality. These events can then be recorded and analyzed under scientific conditions. Remember, there are many variables to consider, including the power of the spirit, and it is of utmost importance to bear in mind that if inducing a sad memory, you may produce not only a memory event, but a full-blown poltergeist outburst from the spirit itself.

example

While spending time at the residence in which I was conducting my investigation (Al's house), an event occurred which serves to support my observations. One night, just prior to Christmas, Shelby and I were visiting with the couple living in the house, which had a high degree of paranormal activity at the time. We were all sitting in the kitchen. Christmas music was playing in the tape deck, and an old song started to play (*Ave Maria*, by the Fischer Choir). Midway through the song, a child's voice was clearly heard singing along by all present. I believe this was a memory response, triggered by a happy event at that time of year for this particular spirit.

The psychological motivation and involvement with a spirit for this type of experiment is shown in the following procedure:

1) The investigator must attempt to establish the identity of those involved (the deceased), along with as much of their personal history as possible.

2) A collection and documentation must be made of events as they are played out in the haunting.

3) An analysis of all data must be made, so that the probable nature of the message or problem being played out in the events can be determined.

4) The best manner in which to proceed must be established. This is the time that the investigator will prepare a psychological event that will deeply involve the individual spirit, with particular attention to the displayed events, or what seems to be important to the spirit.

5) The location of the experiment should be controlled in the following manner:

a) Seal the area to keep unwanted noise out.

b) Ensure that no unauthorized persons can enter the environment.

c) Shut off all unneeded electrical equipment.

d) Set up monitoring equipment within the target area. This equipment should have the ability to be activated by remote.

e) No one, not even the investigator, should remain in the target area once the experiment commences.

6) Begin the scenario, recording all data from the target area

NOTE: To change the events and initiate an interactive response, the investigator can create a psychological problem or solution for the observed events. The investigator must exercise extreme caution in this type of experiment, as a benign situation may quickly develop into a highly active event and/or a full-blown poltergeist event. The three greatest attributes required by the investigator are perseverance, respect for the deceased, and caution.

I wondered about the incident where the malevolent spirit seemed compelled to capture the girl. Up until that point, he seemed to have a difficult time with our equipment operating in the house, which appeared to frustrate him severely. However, after apparently capturing the girl, he displayed a working knowledge of the equipment and tampered with it quite effectively.

If spirits are limited to information, especially technical information, of the era of their deaths, as indicated by the actions of this spirit, it would indicate that the information had to be taught to him by the girl, and not learned through his observation of us operating the equipment. He always knew when and where our systems were operating, but didn't tamper with any of them at first. Does this indicate that sight, as we know it, is hampered in some way in their state? If so, how do they know when we are present and, more specifically, how do they tell one individual from another? Is it possible that they have a keen sense that enables them to feel energy and electromagnetic fields?

To fully understand what I was dealing with, I had to put away my ideologies regarding what death was, and how I perceived reality. This was very important, as our perception of reality clouds our minds, making it impossible to accept the idea of the existence of things whose nature is unknown to us. I went right back to the basics.

As religion became global, there emerged two distinct beliefs. First, that there was a supreme being, and secondly, that an everlasting soul existed. If this is true, then if a soul is to be detected, and the soul is the life force, then the first step to finding the soul is to hunt ghosts — not of the dead, but within the living. The search must start with us. Neuroscience has made wonderful progress in the last ten years, with various discoveries, yet there is a great deal about our brains that modern science knows nothing about.

If the millions of reports of hauntings indicate that life in some form continues after physical death, and if this continuance is what we call the soul, and this soul has the means to appear in sight and sound before the living, then the soul, and those abilities, should logically exist in each one of us prior to our physical deaths. I cannot believe that the soul is created as a result of death, but rather that it is released from the body upon death, and is merely an extension of our being. So if we assume for a moment that our souls reside within us during our lives, then is it not possible that modern scientists have already seen and measured it on many of their sophisticated instruments, perhaps overlooking it as something that is simply life itself? So what would it look like? Some form of energy? More importantly, how would it communicate?

I began examining and comparing several phenomena, looking for clues to this perplexing question. I didn't want to attempt to reinvent the wheel at this point, so I started searching the stacks of existing research from the fields of medicine, parapsychology, and metaphysics.

This research led me to my next project, Project Switch.

project switch

Project switch was started in an attempt to discover the frequencies of life and death and, if they were found, to determine how we could access these frequencies by finding a way to switch them on and off at will.

Deathbed visions: a mountain of research has been conducted on deathbed visions, where the critically ill have reportedly been visited by what are described as deceased friends and relatives. They have been witnessed acknowledging unseen people and answering unheard questions. Witnesses have sometimes described feeling a presence in the room while this was taking place. These events usually take place hours or minutes prior to death. It has been noted that after these episodes, the individual moves into a phase of peace, with reduced pain and an apparent acceptance of their impending demise. The most important information that I found is the rare clinical data compiled on this subject, which shows that while these events take place, the individual's brainwave patterns show low delta waves on the right side of the brain only.

Dreaming: Science has yet to understand dreams and the dreaming process. Sleep studies show that some people will talk or sleepwalk as their brainwave patterns remain in the delta waves. As their brain patterns move slightly into the theta stage, dreaming begins. This has been described as the right side of the brain talking to itself.

Paradoxical sleep is when the brain is actually more active than that of a fully awake and active person. This is also known as REM sleep.

Dream communication: These are usually warnings of something that is about to take place. Action from the recipient is required. The origins of these communications is unknown; some believe that it is spirit guides communicating, while others believe that these messages are coming from a different reality from our own.

Dream telepathy: This is where a person located in a remote room or building concentrates on an image, and attempts to send this information to a person who is asleep. Many experiments, under controlled and monitored conditions, have been conducted on dream telepathy. They reveal that there is great success in this form of communication. The individual who receives the information is normally in the paradoxical sleep pattern.

Out-of-body experience: In this experiment, the subject was monitored in a sleep chamber with EEG equipment. The experiment lasted several hours, which demonstrated clearly that the subject's brain patterns showed high activity within the right side and within the delta–theta border. The subject described retrieved information upon waking that they did not have access to prior to the test.

Experiment One: Well-documented psychic, USA. The subject entered the hospital and met the doctor prior to testing. The subject was taken to a lab where he was attached to various machines, one of which was an EEG. Over the course of a few hours, various tests were conducted which showed the subject to be within the standard baseline conditions.

The next phase began by having several people brought into the room, one at a time, to be read by the psychic; these were all people that the subject had never met before and that he knew nothing about. The subject conducted readings for each of the people, with astonishingly accurate details regarding people who were close to them that had died. The most interesting part of the experiment was that while each reading was taking place, the EEG showed higher than usual activity in the right side of the subject's brain. Even though the subject was fully awake and active, the EEG showed theta and borderline delta brainwave patterns. After each reading, the subject's brainwave patterns would return to normal. This activity could not be explained by the doctor.

Experiment Two: Well-documented psychic, Japan. The subject entered the hospital and met the staff and doctors. She was connected to a wide array of equipment, and tested to ensure that her physical and medical conditions were within normal parameters, which they were. The subject was introduced to a person that she had never met before and commenced her reading of this person. The subject's left brain shut down, and the right brain went into theta and borderline delta wave patterns.

If these two psychics show normal brainwave patterns at all times, with the exception of when they engage in readings (during which their brainwave patterns change drastically, allowing them to establish an open line of communication with the other side), then the switch must be located within the right side of the brain. If we look at all the available data, we should be able to isolate the frequency range.

I wanted to develop a device that would not only find and isolate the location of a spirit, but would also establish open, constant, and consistent communication with them. My first step was to try to find out what it was that I was looking for, so that when I found it, I would recognize it. I approached a senior lab technician, working out of a government institution that I was associated with, and gave him a basic description of what I was looking for. Within thirty minutes he had rigged a simulator, using a frequency analyzer to replicate what the bottom end of the hertz spectrum would sound like. As he queued in the frequencies, he hit one in particular, and I told him to stop. I had heard this sound before. This was the same annoying sound I had heard on several of my control tapes made in the house that contained paranormal activity — like a dull, throbbing headache, the blood pounding out beats in your temples — and it fell directly within the parameters of the data that I had collected.

I had to find out why, in a room full of people, only a single person would hear something unusual, or two people would hear completely different things. I went back to the tapes made in the house, focussing on the tapes that were recorded while I was present. Even though I had heard nothing, voices, sounds, and even conversations were captured on some of these tapes. I took my problem to a colleague, who was a senior electronics lab technician, and who had many years of experience in the navy as an electronics and communications expert. I explained the problem, and he explained that some tape recorders are equipped with a frequency, or phase modulation system, called pre-emphasis, which can pick up sounds beyond our normal hearing and boost them to a frequency that we can hear.

The next test was to have him inspect the tapes using an audio frequency spectrum analyzer, in an attempt to isolate the original incoming frequency.

White noise is the combination of a spectrum of frequencies with equal amplitude (power) per frequency (hertz). It is caused mainly by molecular changes in solids, liquids, and gases within our environment by means of temperature fluctuations or electrical discharges within our atmospheric environment.

We communicate via speech by forcing air from our lungs up through the larynx; the vocal cords constrict and vibrate, creating sounds. But how could we communicate without this physical equipment? Assume that a spirit is detectable by a gauss meter and has a slight range of electromagnetic energy, which can cause air to move and causes changes in temperature, but cannot produce verbal sounds within our hearing range. What if a verbal communication was sent, not from rushing air and constricting vocal cords, but rather from an electrical discharge riding within the ever-present white noise?

The human ear is a complex mechanism. Within the ear is an organ called the Corti, which contains thousands of hair cells. When a wave or a burst of energy passes over these hairs, it causes them to move, which sends impulses to the cochlear nerve and then onto the cerebral cortex.

The brain then interprets the information received. Could a silent burst of energy bypass the outer ear and cause the corti to detect and transfer information to the brain? It would depend greatly upon how agitated the environment became. Subtle messages would require electronic assistance, such as a tape recorder. The pre-emphasis chip captures sound outside the normal hearing range and boosts its signal into the audible range.

An independent study of the audio surveillance tapes tested on an audio frequency analyzer came back with very interesting results. Communications captured on these tapes were all at twenty-two hertz, at the low end of human hearing, but what was interesting was the decibel range — clear messages at twenty-two hertz were at minus forty-one and forty-two decibels. Those messages captured that were not as clear were still at twenty-two hertz, with a decibel range of minus forty-six to minus fifty-one. Further, there was indication of more communications at twenty-two hertz with a decibel range so far below zero that it was impossible to enhance. This range was found to be between minus seventy-six and minus one hundred and thirteen decibels.

electronic voice phenomena in relation to white noise

magnetic recording tape

electronic voice phenomena

I AM HERE

amplitude

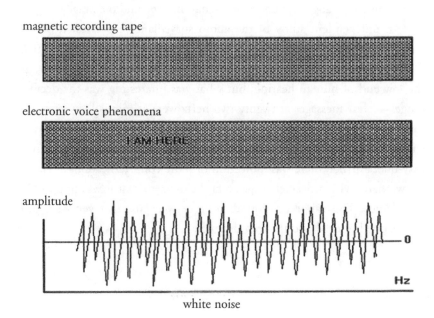

0

Hz

white noise

glossary

Brainwave States:
beta: awake and active, 30 to 14 cycles per second.
alpha: deep relaxation, 13 to 8 cycles per second.
theta: drowsiness, 7 to 4 cycles per second.
delta: deep sleep/unconsciousness, 3.5 to 0.5 cycles per second.
Deathbed visions: Just prior to death, when visions occur, brain patterns show delta waves on the right side of the brain only.
Dreaming: Essentially, the right brain talking to itself.
Dream telepathy: Right brain delta waves.
EEG (electroencephalogram): Can record electrical brainwaves. These patterns from different areas of the brain can then be studied.
Frequency: The number of vibrations, oscillations, or cycles in a unit time; normally in one-second intervals.
OBE (out-of-body experience): Low theta brainwave activity.
Psychic 1: Right brain theta/delta waves.
Psychic 2: Right brain theta/delta waves.

Encounters:
One: Sensing or feeling the presence of spirits.
Two: Sounds, smells, unexplained cold areas in warm rooms.
Three: Witnessing the aftereffects of poltergeist activities.
Four: Seeing a spirit.
Five: Occupying the same space at the same time as a spirit.
Six: Interaction with a spirit, or having a spirit manipulate events in your life.

annex i: at time of death

Content:	Not content:	Obsessive:
At peace, fulfilled, sense of completeness. Passive observation.	Wants more, lacking sense of fulfillment, unfinished business. Active observation; attempts to influence the living. Involuntary memory manifestation. Interaction: Helpful, protective. Frustration: Sounds of glass breaking with no physical evidence of the occurrences.	Feels angry, guilty, victimized, greedy; holds religious belief that more suffering is to come for past deeds. Active observation, attempts to influence the living. Involuntary memory manifestation. Interaction: Attempts to continue routine of past life within our reality. Attempts to manipulate our actions. Communication: Insertion, dreams/nightmares. Missing items, moving objects, lights and appliances turned on and off. Sense of being able to communicate with the living. Missing or ignoring messages offered. Frustration: Physical damage done. Attacks on people and animals. Refusal to accept responsibility for actions.

witness statements

Witness Statement 1

"My friend and I were talking, and he mentioned that some strange occurrences were happening at his house, where a former tenant had killed herself. One day we were sitting in the living room; there was no one else in the house, and we were both being very quiet; within a few minutes we heard running upstairs. I asked him who was there, and he said that no one else was home, and that those were the sounds that he had been hearing. Almost every time I went over to his house I heard running and stomping.

"One night my wife and I went over for dinner. We were sitting at the table when I saw a flash of light. I looked over at my wife and asked if she had seen the light. She said that she had.

"Shortly after that incident, my friend asked to borrow my camcorder. We set it up at the end of the hallway in his bedroom, aimed it toward the bathroom, and let it record overnight. The next day we watched the video, and I noticed shadows running up and down the hallway. At the end of the tape, the bathroom door, which was closed, flew open, and a shadowy figure could be seen batting at the shower curtain.

"Now whenever I go over to his house it feels as though someone is watching me, and I feel a cold presence."

J. Modine,
Al's neighbour.

Witness Statement 2

"My wife told me that she was over at her friend's house when she heard running and banging, and what sounded like furniture moving. She explained that other than herself and the woman that she was visiting, there was no one else in the house. The next time she went over I tagged along. As soon as I walked in, I felt a heavy pressure trying to push me down, and an uneasy feeling came over me. I didn't like the feeling of that place. It was a few weeks later when their neighbor told me about an event that took place involving his wife the previous night. It was described to me as being almost like a war zone.

"Curiosity took me back to the house. I met Al, and he told me what had happened and took me for a tour. I saw the after-effects of what looked like a fight, or some sort of a struggle. There were drag marks from boot heels; the strange thing is that these marks continued under the furniture as if it wasn't there. I also noticed a smudged handprint on the wall. It was all very disturbing."

T.S.,
Family friend.

Witness Statement 3
"I have lived next door for two years; I knew the previous tenants, and I know the new tenants as well. On many occasions when I went over, I heard strange noises and saw weird things happen. For example, one night as I entered the house, I noticed that everyone seemed on-edge, but since they knew that I was not extremely comfortable with the situation, they didn't mention anything. I sat on a footstool near the closet, and we all proceeded to watch a video. All of a sudden, the door behind me flew open and slammed into the wall. Everyone jumped. There was no one there. I was extremely frightened and ran out of the house.

"On several occasions I've heard footsteps, furniture moving, and voices. On one occasion I heard whistling."

Kalena Modine,
Al's neighbour.

Witness Statement 4
"One afternoon I went over to pick up my son. Kellie wasn't back from picking up her daughter from school and she had taken my son with her. I let myself in and waited for her to return. I heard noises upstairs and I believed that Al was home. These noises were of walking, running water,

and the toilet flushing. Regular bathroom noises. A few minutes later I looked out the front of the house to see if Kellie was coming back yet. I saw Al outside. I told him about what I had heard. There was no one up there."

Susan,
Family friend.

Witness Statement 5
"I entered the house and immediately had an uneasy feeling, as if I wasn't welcome there. I didn't like the feeling, as it made me uncomfortable. We sat in the kitchen for a few minutes until I felt that we could move on. We started up the stairs and a feeling of panic hit me; I had to get out of there, so I turned and went right out the front door. We stood out in the street for a while talking about the house. I felt better outside.

"Later that day, we went over to the store. As we passed the courtyard, I spotted a man leaning out an open window in the main house[12]. He seemed strange to me, as he was obscured by shadow even though the sun was bright. He wore an old-style hat, and seemed to stare at me. I bought my pop, excused myself, and went home."

George S.,
Family friend.

endnotes

1   The belief that upon death one is greeted by deceased family or friends to help them to move on. This belief is re-enforced by deathbed observations, reports by those about to die, and from people who have had near death experiences.

2   The owner, after suffering great injustice, was in time found to be completely innocent. The charges were dropped, and he returned to his family and his mansion.

3   This noise was also captured on the tape recordings made by Richard Winer and Nancy Osborn during their investigation of the Miami Biltmore Hotel. (*Haunted Houses*, Bantam, 1979)

4   There is a classic theory that past events can be imprinted onto an environment, which when triggered plays over and over like a video loop.

5   Nielson, Greg and Polansky, Joseph. *Pendulum Power*. Destiny Books, 1990.

6   Audio signals outside of our normal hearing seem to be a tool that the spirits used to their advantage. I believe, through reports and personal observations, that these "sound insertions," as I call them, are not received via normal hearing functions, and that by bypassing our hearing and placing sounds or voices directly into our brains they can target individuals or specific groups of people and have them hear exactly what they want them to hear, thus activating or influencing a response. This was seen many times as one or two people in a group heard things that others did not. It was also used when the women were called simultaneously to the stairs, and it was effectively used in this situation.

7   Of the fourteen people listed under that surname in the city telephone directory, one was listed at the address given to us.

8   Original owner awarded the property by the colony.

9   Referring to a local park approximately two and a half miles from the location of the house.

10 A gangster in the 1930s who operated an illegal gaming house not far from the estate.

11 The courtyard is designed as a Celtic cross with a large fountain in the centre.

12 The window indicated by the witness was the attic window; that area of the house was vacant and locked at the time. This spirit in the top hat has been seen twice more by different witnesses.